Teaching Business English

Also published in
Oxford Handbook for Language Teachers

Teaching English Overseas: An Introduction
Sandra Lee McKay

Teaching American English Pronunciation
Peter Avery and Susan Ehrlich

How Languages are Learned
Patsy M. Lightbown and Nina Spada

Teaching
Business English

Mark Ellis and Christine Johnson

Oxford University Press 1994

Oxford University Press
Walton Street, Oxford OX2 6DP

Oxford New York
Athens Auckland Bangkok Bombay
Calcutta Cape Town Dar es Salaam Delhi
Florence Hong Kong Istanbul Karachi
Kuala Lumpur Madras Madrid Melbourne
Mexico City Nairobi Paris Singapore
Taipei Tokyo Toronto

and associated companies in
Berlin Ibadan

Oxford and *Oxford English* are trade marks of
Oxford University Press

ISBN 0 19 437167 0

© Mark Ellis and Christine Johnson 1994

First published 1994
Second impression 1995

Set in Adobe Garamond
by Wyvern Typesetting, Bristol
Printed in Hong Kong

CONTENTS

PART TWO: **Analysing the needs of the learners**

11 Framework materials

12 Authentic materials

13 Managing activities in the classroom

ACKNOWLEDGEMENTS

The Publisher and Authors would like to thank the following for their kind permission to use articles, extracts, or adaptations from copyright material.

Activity and diagram from 'Corporate language training in the 1990s' by A. Pilbeam in *Language and Intercultural Training*, published by LTS Training and Consulting.

Functioning in Business by P. Knowles, F. Bailey, and R. Jillet, published by Longman Group 1991.

Business Objectives by V. Hollett, published by Oxford University Press 1991.

'How a streamlined logistics system can make all the difference', *International Management* October 1984.

Make Your Own Language Tests by B. Carroll and P. Hall, published by Pergamon Press 1985.

Unisys Limited for an extract from the computer manual for *Offis Manager*.

Bill Reed for the list of Business textbooks, originally compiled for BESIG members.

Diagram from *Educational English Teacher's Resource Book* by W. Reed and S. Nolan, published by Longman 1992.

Business Targets by S. Greenall, published by Heinemann Publishers (Oxford) 1986.

LTS for an extract from *Systems One*.

United Paper Mills, Finland, for permission to refer to their Language Ability Scale.

Cartoons by Sophie Grillet © Oxford University Press 1994.

INTRODUCTION

This book is aimed at teachers, trainers, and course organizers who are working or intending to work with:

- Job-experienced language learners from companies or other business institutions: managers, office staff, and other professionals such as lawyers and engineers.

- Pre-experience language learners studying, for example, Business Studies or Trade and Commerce at schools, colleges, or universities.

Objectives

The main objective is to provide readers with a practical approach to the teaching of Business English. In order to do this, the book gives relevant background about business learners, the world they work in, and the language they use. It also presents strategies for teachers approaching the training task:

- How to become better informed

- How to define the objectives of training

- How to prepare materials and activities for the classroom

- How to evaluate performance and progress.

We think it is important to put the learner at the centre of the teaching process. With professional, job-experienced learners, this means exploiting their knowledge and experience both for content and as a source of motivation. Pre-experience learners may not have the same hands-on experience of business procedures, but they do have a developing knowledge of business theory and standard practices, and, presumably, an interest in business topics which can be very valuable in the language learning classroom.

Content

The book is divided into three parts.

Part One gives a general background to the subject and is intended mainly for people who are new to Business English teaching or who may be thinking about moving into the profession.

Part Two focuses on the needs of the learners and demonstrates how a teacher can analyse these needs in order to determine the shape and content of a course. Chapter 7, however, is specifically concerned with job analysis—an area not as directly relevant to pre-experience learners on business courses at universities and commercial schools as it is for those already at work.

Part Three looks at materials and activities. It gives some pointers about how to select materials and how to develop materials and activities for the classroom. It also makes suggestions about classroom management and strategies for dealing with different kinds of learners.

Parts Two and Three are intended to provide ideas for practising teachers and experienced teachers, as well as offering guidance to newcomers.

The terms 'training' and 'trainer' are frequently used throughout this book to refer to the process of acquiring business communication skills and to the person running the courses. Particularly in the context of company language learning, these terms are felt to be more accurate than 'teaching' or 'teacher'. 'Training' is the word commonly used to refer to what adults receive in a company context: we talk, for example, about management training, computer training, and sales training. Teaching, on the other hand, implies education: the passing on of knowledge, but also of a right and wrong way of doing things. It more properly describes what young people receive in school, and may in some cases have bad connotations for businesspeople. Another implication of 'teaching' is that it involves giving information about the system of the language, whereas 'training' implies developing skills in using language as a means of communication. Current approaches to the conducting of Business English courses reflect this emphasis on skills and performance, as will be seen in Chapter 5.

PART ONE

Introduction to Business English

1 WHAT IS BUSINESS ENGLISH?

Background

In the last two decades, Business English has attracted increasing interest and awareness. Business English courses are offered by many language schools worldwide (by over 100 schools in the UK alone); there are more than 150 Business English titles on UK publishers' lists; examining boards offer Business English examinations; the Business English Special Interest Group (part of IATEFL, the International Association for Teachers of English as a Foreign Language) has over 1500 members from around the world. Yet despite this enormous interest, Business English is an area often neglected by linguistic researchers, who prefer to work on other—more easily defined—areas of special English.

Business English must be seen in the overall context of English for Specific Purposes (ESP), as it shares the important elements of needs analysis, syllabus design, course design, and materials selection and development which are common to all fields of work in ESP. As with other varieties of ESP, Business English implies the definition of a specific language corpus and emphasis on particular kinds of communication in a specific context.

However, Business English differs from other varieties of ESP in that it is often a mix of specific content (relating to a particular job area or industry), and general content (relating to general ability to communicate more effectively, albeit in business situations).

There have been many developments in the ways in which teachers and course designers look at Business English. In the late 1960s and early 1970s, specialist vocabulary was seen to be what distinguished Business English from General English, and there was a preoccupation with business-related words and terminology. Earlier textbooks—such as *British Banking* by J. Firth in the Peter Stevens series, published by Cassell in 1971—reflect this approach. The principle underlying these earliest Business English coursebooks was to present target specialist vocabulary in the context of a written text or dialogue which dealt with a particular topic (for example, in *British Banking*, exchange and exchange control, companies and their bank accounts). Exercises consisted mainly of comprehension questions on the text, vocabulary exercises, and the drilling of randomly selected structures. It was assumed that the learner had already studied the language to at least intermediate level. On the other hand, any existing knowledge of the subject was not taken into account: in fact, the expository nature of the texts assumed that the learner had little knowledge. There was no consideration of how the learner might apply the language in real life, and no development of skills such as interacting in meetings or writing letters

A second approach, heralded by the BBC/OUP video and coursebook *English for Business* (also known as *The Bellcrest File*), published in 1972, placed a greater emphasis on training 'the skills of communication in English speaking, writing, listening and reading within a business context' (quoted from the Introduction to the Teacher's Book). The course included development of listening skills (based on working with the video), structural drills, gambit drills, dialogue practice, and role simulations. Again, it assumed that the learners had already covered the fundamental grammar of English, but that they needed to continue to develop their knowledge in order to handle practical situations effectively. Whilst still very much a reflection of the structural/audio-lingual approach to language teaching, *English for Business* was a flagship course in the development of Business English teaching.

In the mid-1970s and 1980s, following the trends in General English, Business English teaching began to focus more and more on functional areas—formulaic language for recommending, giving opinions, showing agreement, and so on. This kind of teaching was supported by lists of 'gambits' derived from the Kellor corpus from Canada. An example of a functionally-orientated coursebook for Business English is *Functioning in Business* by Knowles and Bailey (Longman, 1987). In the original edition, this course presented listening practice at a pre-intermediate level on cassette, exemplifying key language for making appointments, confirming plans, introductions, business lunches, and so on. The conversations on cassette were followed up by functional language practice (for example, requesting, agreeing, clarifying) and role play.

Since the late 1980s, Business English teaching has drawn on aspects of all the previous approaches, but also places much more emphasis on the need to develop the skills for using the language learned.

The development of company training programmes during the 1980s began to provide employees with opportunities to attend courses in presentation techniques, negotiating, and effective meetings skills, among other things. This led to the publication of books and materials on business skills, and these were also available to Business English teachers, course designers, and materials developers. The recognition of the need for businesspeople to be proficient in business communication skills has had a major impact on Business English teaching. Although it is not the designated brief of the Business English teacher to train businesspeople in behavioural techniques (for example, presentation or negotiation), it is hard to ignore the influence that good behavioural skills have on successful communication. Many job-experienced learners now come to the language course to learn to perform in English, tasks that they can already perform in their mother tongue. In other cases, however, pre-experience language learners may need training in behavioural skills, and in colleges and business schools there is now a wide acceptance of the need to start training learners in, for example, basic presentation techniques.

This approach to Business English teaching is reflected in coursebooks such as Vicki Hollett's *Business Objectives* (Oxford University Press, 1991), which bases language practice activities around the key communication skills areas.

Today there are many varieties of Business English. The most important distinction to be made is that between pre-experience (or low-experience) learners and job-experienced learners. Students in colleges or universities will have gained their knowledge of business largely from books and, as a result, such knowledge will be incomplete and theoretical rather than practical. They will be less aware of their language needs in terms of communicating in real-life business situations, and their expectations of language learning will be moulded by their experiences from school, and thus by the educational policies of the country in which they grew up.

Job-experienced learners will also be influenced by their educational backgrounds, but they will, in most cases, have gained some practical experience of having to communicate on the job. This experience has the effect of focusing their attention on what they perceive as their own shortcomings in terms of fluency, getting the message across, and being able to understand the people from other countries that they have to deal with.

Pre-experience learners will have two kinds of needs: (1) Their present situation may require them to read textbooks in English or follow lectures in English in order to gain the qualifications they are seeking. A major component of their English training may therefore be the development of reading and listening skills, with a strong emphasis on the vocabulary of the subject. In addition (depending on where they are studying), they may have to attend seminars or write papers in English. These will then constitute important skills objectives for any language training programme they follow. (2) They will need to prepare for their future working life in business. In this regard, their teachers may include in their language course such skills as commercial correspondence, participating in meetings, or presenting information or social interactions, depending on the kind of jobs they are preparing for.

Job-experienced learners are more likely to have a single set of needs relating to their job. Sometimes learners may need English for a new job or a situation which they have not yet experienced (for example, an employee who is about to be posted abroad) and, in these cases, they will not know very precisely what needs they are going to have. However, one overriding characteristic of Business English for job-experienced learners will still apply: the need to be pragmatic. The practical *use* of the language will be more important than theoretical knowledge *about* the language. The employee who has been selected for a new job or a new project will have to be able to manage in spite of his or her incomplete knowledge or inadequate skills, and providing strategies for coping will be an essential feature of a language course for such a person.

There is a third important distinction between courses for pre-experience and job-experienced learners. Pre-experience learners are in many cases preparing for examinations. If these are to be taken in English, the examination curriculum will provide the basis for the syllabus and will set out very specific objectives for the course; it will not be left to the teacher or the learners to decide for themselves what they will do.

In the case of job-experienced learners, the objectives for the course and its content will be the product of a negotiating process between the learner (or sponsoring organization) and the trainer (or training organization). The learning parameters are flexible and perhaps even vague, and it is more difficult to assess in precise terms the success of training.

Within the two main areas of pre-experience and job-experienced Business English teaching, there are also many varieties.

The kinds of English courses offered by colleges and universities will vary widely depending on the level of qualification the students are aiming at and the types of work they will later be engaged in. The needs of students following vocational courses in, say, commercial practice (import–export) or secretarial training will be vastly different from those following a university degree course in Business Administration. The differences will be evident in the level of language and the kinds of language knowledge and language skills required.

Similarly, courses for job-experienced learners will differ in objectives, course content, and methodology—depending on the type of business the learners are involved in, their jobs and job requirements, the length of the course, and the structure of the learner group. Individual tuition implies more precisely defined objectives and a more flexible approach to method-ology and use of materials compared to group tuition.

These varieties of Business English and their implications for course plan-ning and implementation will be discussed in more depth throughout the book.

What characterizes the language of business?

As mentioned earlier, Business English is an area of ESP that is relatively poorly researched. Rigorous linguistic analysis is fragmented and is more frequently based on the written forms of language such as correspondence, annual reports, and articles in business journals. Some kinds of analysis have been carried out with respect to the language of meetings and discus-sions, but there is still little to support course developers beyond their own first-hand experience gained in the field.

What follows is our own understanding of what Business English is, based on many years of working with a wide range of pre-experience and especially job-experienced learners.

Sense of purpose

The most important characteristic of exchanges in the context of business meetings, telephone calls, and discussions is a sense of purpose. Language is used to achieve an end, and its successful use is seen in terms of a suc-cessful outcome to the business transaction or event. Users of Business English need to speak English primarily so that they can achieve more in their jobs. Business is competitive: competition exists between companies and also within companies, between employees striving to better their careers. It follows that performance objectives take priority over educa-tional objectives or language learning for its own sake. For example, a German company in Seoul may have a long-term objective to establish good trading relations, and their representative's use of English is geared to that end. A French telecommunications project manager in India needs to know English to communicate with his technical teams on the site, who are all Indian. A Swedish pharmaceutical product manager needs to give clear presentations of recent product development to subsidiaries in Europe and the Far East. In each of these examples, the use of language has an implied element of risk: mistakes and misunderstandings could cost the company dearly.

Much of the language needed by businesspeople (apart from social lan-guage) will be transactional: getting what you want and persuading others to agree with the course of action you propose. The language will frequently be objective rather than subjective and personal. For example, in discussions and meetings, it will be more appropriate to evaluate facts from an objective standpoint ('This is a positive point', 'On the other hand the disadvantage is . . .') rather than expressing personal feelings and opinions.

Social aspects

International businesspeople have a need to make contact with others whom they have never met before, or know only slightly. Meetings are often short because businesspeople are always pressed for time. There is a need for an internationally accepted way of doing things so that people from different cultures, and with different mother tongues, can quickly feel more comfortable with one another.

Social contacts are often highly ritualized. Formulaic language is used (in greetings and introductions, for example) in the context of a routine pattern of exchanges. A certain style is generally adopted which is polite but also short and direct (taking into consideration the need to be economical with time). Although some situations may require more than this (for example, keeping a conversation going over lunch), the style and content of social interactions will be typified by a desire to build a good relationship while avoiding over-familiarity.

Clear communication

Information has to be conveyed with minimum risk of misunderstanding, and the time for processing (both by the speaker and by the listener) needs to be short. Therefore there is a preference for clear, logical, thought emphasized by the kinds of words that indicate the logical process (for example, 'as a result', 'for this reason', 'in order to'). There is often a need to be concise—particularly when communicating by fax or telephone—and certain familiar concepts may be expressed in word clusters to avoid circumlocution (for example, 'cash with order', 'just in time delivery'). Certain terms have evolved to save time in referring to concepts which people in business are familiar with (for example, 'primary industry', 'parent company'). Many of these are acronyms (for example, CIF and FOB).

The Business English syllabus

People around the world conduct business meetings in English even though English may be a foreign language to all those present. The language that they use will be neither as rich in vocabulary and expression, nor as culture-bound, as that used by native speakers, but will be based on a core of the most useful and basic structures and vocabulary. Businesspeople do not always need to know the full complexities of English grammar and idiom. Fine distinctions in meaning (as are conveyed by some of the compound tenses, for example) may not be important in a business context. On the other hand, in a Business English course some structural areas may require more attention than in a conventional course: for example, conditionals in negotiating, or modality for expressing possibility or politeness. There is consequently a need for syllabus designers to be selective when addressing the needs of Business English learners.

The Business English syllabus is likely to be defined primarily in relation to business performance skills such as meetings, presentations, socializing, or report-writing. Within these skills areas, certain concepts are typically discussed and expressed: for example, describing changes and trends, quality, product, process and procedures, strategy. These concepts can be broken down into the more linguistically powerful functional areas such as comparing and contrasting, expressing cause and effect, recommending, and agreeing. The language defined in the syllabus may include grammatical or lexical items, and elements of spoken or written discourse, including, for instance, cohesive devices and stress and intonation patterns, as well as organizational features such as signalling a new topic or turn-taking in interactive sequences.

There is no single description of what a Business English syllabus might consist of, although many coursebooks do present a generally-accepted common core of functions, structures, and vocabulary.

Business and General English courses

Not all courses run by a company or a business college necessarily merit the title of 'Business English'. Some companies and colleges provide language courses where needs have not been analysed and the course content is drawn from a General English coursebook. It may be that a choice has been made to improve the general command of English of the participants, and that this then constitutes the course objective. On the other hand, such a course may be the result of a lack of informed strategy on the part of the company or institution, or a lack of expertise on the part of available trainers.

As we showed in the first half of this chapter, Business English is not a neatly-defined category of special English. The term is used to cover a variety of Englishes, some of which are very specific, and some very general. The table below makes some general statements about key differences between Business and General English; however, we acknowledge that there are many situations where the distinctions are not so clear.

Table 1.1: Business English v. General English—a summary

Pre-course preparation	Business English	General English
Needs analysis	To assess the needs of the company, the job, and the individuals, and to define the language level required by the job. In-company training departments must make decisions about the type of training required: group v. individual, on-site v. language school, person-to-person tuition v. distance learning, etc.	To assess the language needs of the learners.
Assessment of level	Using formal tests or interviews.	Placement tests or interviews to allocate learners to courses or to form groups of a similar language level.

Pre-course preparation	Business English	General English
Syllabus	Set courses will have <u>fixed objectives and syllabus.</u> Special courses will require a special syllabus. One-to-one courses may develop syllabus and content on an ongoing basis.	Often determined by choice of coursebook and (if applicable) an end-of-course examination. The syllabus is wide-ranging and may encompass the broad vocabulary and variety of styles found in literature and other general reading and in the world of entertainment and the media.
Course objectives	Defined precisely in relation to the needs analysis findings. May be worded in terms of the <u>tasks/skills required in the job</u> (job-experienced learners) <u>or course of study</u> (pre-experience learners), <u>or in terms of required language improvement</u> (e.g. command of structures or pronunciation).	Examination courses (e.g. Cambridge First Certificate) will have fixed pre-determined objectives. Individuals may have their own objectives: interest in the culture; desire to travel or live abroad; a feeling that language skills will be useful or will lead to better job prospects.
Time	In company language training, there are usually time constraints because of the need for training to be cost-effective. In colleges and universities, time for language study is also likely to be limited.	Outside the state education system, general language study will usually be open-ended. Even examinations can be repeated if necessary. An exception would be someone preparing for a holiday or residence abroad.
Learner expectations	Learners are likely to be more goal-orientated and to expect success. Business people normally have high expectations of efficiency, quality, and professionalism.	Learners also want to make progress but are less likely to set themselves specific targets within a rigid timescale.

Table 1.1: Continued

Pre-course preparation	Business English	General English
Materials	Print, audio, and video materials can be bought off the shelf for Business English—but they may not meet the specific needs of an individual or group. It may be necessary to develop materials for a specific course.	In most parts of the world, there is now a wide choice of off-the-shelf materials for General English teaching at all levels. Materials development by the teacher is not usually required or expected.
Methodology	Many learning tasks and activities will be the same as on a General English course, especially for teaching structures, vocabulary, and social English. Role-plays are common to both although the situations and language will differ. Business English also borrows ideas from management training—e.g. problem-solving, decision-making, and team-building tasks. Job-experienced learners will be given many opportunities to present and discuss aspects of their work.	There may be a broader range of techniques in use in the General English classroom. Many activities are designed to make learning more 'fun', and variety for its own sake is important to maintain interest and motivation in the absence of specific needs.

Pre-course preparation	Business English	General English
Evaluation of progress	In colleges and universities there may be set (written and oral) examinations. In company language training there is usually no examination, but the training organization may use an off-the-shelf Business English test. In informal assessment, the emphasis is usually on evaluating the success of communication—i.e. did the speaker/writer express the idea precisely enough and appropriately enough for the target situation?	Formal examinations include a written paper in which marks are awarded for grammatical accuracy as well as range of vocabulary and appropriacy. Oral examinations also take into account fluency, pronunciation and general communicative ability. Informal assessment (e.g. of class performance) is likely to focus mainly on grammatical accuracy, appropriacy of vocabulary and expression and pronunciation.

2 WHO WANTS TO LEARN BUSINESS ENGLISH?

Pre-experience learners

The major differences between those learners who have had job experience and those who have not has been shown in Chapter 1. Those who have not are usually in the educational system—either in special Commercial Colleges at high school level, where ages might, as in Italy, be as low as sixteen or seventeen—or at an undergraduate or postgraduate level, at universities such as Graz and Klagenfurt in Austria, the European Business Schools, the Higher Colleges of Technology in Dubai, the Schools of Economics in Stockholm and Helsinki, the Asian Institute of Technology in Bangkok, and universities and colleges in the United Kingdom such as the Manchester Business School.

Some colleges may specialize in vocational training for mature students, such as the unemployed or mothers returning to work. An example of this is AFPA in France. Language courses in these colleges will often precede or run parallel to academic courses, and performance objectives will sometimes be tightly linked to the academic syllabus and course content. Business English for such students is orientated towards learning subject matter as well as language. Commercial students in Italy, for example, have specially written English textbooks which in part contain direct information about the banking system, import and export matters such as letters of credit and shipping terms, and company organization and structure.

The reasons for students being at these colleges will be mixed. Some will need to gain a basic business qualification to allow them to work in administration—for example, as clerks and secretaries. In some parts of the world, especially in the Middle East, women will go through a business course, and learn English, but will never expect to go into business at all as marriage often comes first.

In many colleges and universities where business and science or engineering are taught, the students will have the highest aspirations, and expect to go far in their individual careers. Included in this group will be students (at undergraduate or postgraduate level) who go abroad to study. Students from Latin America, Africa, and the Middle East may have the opportunity to follow a Business Studies programme at an American or British university. Most of them will need to improve their language skills before—and also during—their course of academic study and in most cases the Language Department of the college or university in question will be responsible for developing a course for them.

In general, pre-experience learners will be more open-minded than those who are already well ahead in their careers, and this has implications for what can be done in the classroom. However, they may lack confidence in their ability to deal with business subject matter. It is certainly the case, as witnessed by the types of textbooks often used with such learners, that they need to be given a lot of information from which to work.

Low-experience learners

Junior company members

People who are sent on a language course are often high-flyers, but it is important to remember that they are still learning the ways in which their company operates and may not be familiar with what happens outside their own departments or job functions. And while they may have a better command of English than those who are older, they may not have had enough experience to contribute effectively to meetings and negotiations.

In some countries, for example Germany and Switzerland, there may be an apprentice system in which school leavers are taken on by large companies, and are trained in both practical and theoretical aspects of a job (secretarial or clerical). This training may include some language classes where appropriate.

Learners who are moving jobs

Company employees quite frequently move jobs, and often move to other countries, and both these situations may warrant a period of language training. What is important to remember here is that they may know very little about their new job. They cannot give presentations about it because they have little information themselves. A further category here are those people learning English in countries that have only recently adopted western political and economic systems. For such learners it is not only the English language which might be new, but also the systems and procedures of the new political models.

Job-experienced learners

Reasons for learning English

There are countless reasons why a job-experienced company employee might wish to learn English. Here are some examples:

1 A large American multinational in France has English as its company language. Large numbers of employees are in daily contact with native speakers and with members of subsidiaries. Such employees include secretaries, import–export personnel, distribution managers, marketing personnel, engineers, and information technology personnel.

2 A Finnish paper company sells worldwide and has subsidiaries in Europe, including Britain. Its telephone operators, secretaries, sales personnel, factory managers, and engineers all need to speak English.

3 An Italian bank deals on a daily basis with other banks throughout Europe. Its foreign exchange dealers, its computer personnel, and its loan managers come into daily contact with people speaking English.

4 A small businessman in Germany is setting up an import–export company and he needs to travel frequently to the United States, where he will use English for business and socially.

5 A Japanese manager of a German firm is in frequent contact with head office in Düsseldorf. He and his fellow managers need English to telephone and fax the parent company, and to handle visitors from that company when they visit Japan.

6 A Swedish company is in the process of internationalizing, and has decided to use English as a joint company language. It has just taken over two other companies, one of which is in Belgium. Many more members of the company will be travelling than before, and many more will be using English on a regular basis.

Characteristics of the learners

These business learners use language in order to achieve precise objectives. They are likely to apply the same critical standards to language training and training materials as they do elsewhere in their business lives. They are often curious about the objectives of particular tasks. They will be critical of their own performance, and of that of the trainer. Many will ceaselessly evaluate what they are doing, and what is being done. As the learning environment is highly influenced by this sense of purpose, materials, exercises, and activities which are selected for use in the classroom must acknowledge it.

They are also highly aware of time. This is an important factor on intensive courses where learners might be using the opportunity of a lifetime to improve their communicative ability in English, and can place enormous pressure on a course.

The experience of the learner is equally important. Learners come to the language classroom with different experiences—in the world of business, as social human beings, and as learners in other training environments. The businessperson who walks into the classroom on a Monday in order to improve performance while attending international meetings may have had years of experience engaging in meetings and negotiations, and might very well have just come off a training course on computers, time management, or marketing. He or she will judge the materials in the English course with exactly the same thoroughness and sense of expectation that will have been applied to the materials on the marketing course.

The aptitude of the individual may well clash with these three influences, just as it may support them. There are some learners from the business world, as from all backgrounds, who find it difficult to learn another language. They do not recognize the systems, they apply the wrong procedures, and they may have attitudes or learning characteristics which act as a barrier. It follows that the flexibility—even pragmatism—of the trainer in regard to what can be achieved with an individual learner or group of learners will be of crucial importance.

Cultural differences

There are certain cultural differences which the Business English trainer needs to take into account. Many trainers have noticed that in meetings, for example, people from different countries may behave quite differently (a fact also noted at length by John Mole in his book *Mind Your Manners*). In Sweden and the other Nordic countries, participants in meetings pay strict attention to turn-taking, and seldom interrupt. In southern Europe this is not the case. In Britain, making a humorous remark during a presentation is often appreciated. As again noted by John Mole, in Germany this is rarely the case. In Norway, many trainers have noticed that participants in groups are often mutually supportive. The reaction of the group to constant individual criticism will be different to that of groups from other countries—i.e. the group will often feel uncomfortable. In Japan, open confrontation is avoided.

It is equally true that individual companies, such as IBM, may have their own identifiable cultures which leave their mark on their employees. For many businesspeople, therefore, local cultures will probably become less and less dominant as common international business behaviour develops

worldwide. So, while it may be useful to expect that a businessman from Japan will behave as other Japanese businessmen, he might very well have worked in an American company, or lived in the United States, and assumed some of the characteristics of businesspeople from that country.

Cultural similarities and differences, and how they influence what goes well in a class and what does not, are major factors to consider when dealing with the learner. The role of the trainer has also to be considered. In certain cultures, such as those of south and south-east Asia, there is a great power distance between teacher and learner, which means that the learner accepts everything the teacher says and expects him or her to make decisions and to be in control. In other cultures, teacher and learner work closely together: the learner participates in determining the content of the course and is assertive in demanding particular activities. All of the above must be borne in mind when considering comments and suggestions made in the different sections of this book. (For a more detailed discussion about cultural similarities and differences and cross-cultural awareness, see the Suggestions for Further Reading, at the end of the book.)

3 WHERE IS BUSINESS ENGLISH TAUGHT?

Types of institution

Public and private sector educational institutions

This is where the great majority of pre-experience Business English takes place. The range of such institutions is enormous. It includes the Commercial Colleges found throughout the Far East and the Commercial Schools in Italy. It includes the specialist schools of higher education in France, and Schools of Economics and Management in Norway, Sweden, and Finland. In Germany there are large organizations such as the Grone Schule in Hamburg, and Carl Duisberg Centres in Cologne and Hanover where Business English is on offer as part of a much larger package of vocational training. At one level learners can be young and still at high school level, such as those studying in the Italian Commercial Schools. However, there are also job-experienced learners studying in universities and colleges worldwide, including several universities in the United Kingdom, such as Aston, Liverpool, and Newcastle, which are attracting increasing numbers of learners of Business English.

Adult learning centres and Chambers of Commerce

Many native-speaker teachers of Business English work in adult learning centres in Europe, such as the *Volkshochschulen* in Germany and the Chambers of Commerce in Italy and France. The *Kursverksamheten*, ABF, and TBV groups in Sweden, apart from sending teachers into companies, also have learning centres around the country. In France AFPA has centres around the country, and organizes a lot of business language teaching, particularly for secretarial needs.

British Council- and American-sponsored centres

Business English is also taught in many of these centres, for example those in Hong Kong and Bangkok.

Language schools

Business English is taught widely in language schools throughout the world. Schools offering Business English abound in the cities of France, Germany, Spain, Italy, and Scandinavia, and are increasing in places like Budapest, Prague, Warsaw, and St Petersburg.

Japan is a large centre for schools offering Business English, as are the countries of south and south-east Asia—Thailand, Taiwan, and Indonesia. And in language schools in the United Kingdom, Ireland, the United States, and Canada, though General English may form the most important source of income, Business English is becoming increasingly important.

Training and consulting groups and individual consultants

These have come into greater prominence over the last decade. They exist not only in Britain but also in most European countries. They differ from general language schools in that they specialize in Business English, and English for Specific Purposes. The larger groups may have trainers with specialist skills, and may work on several different projects at once. Individual consultants may be tied into a single company, or be limited in their range of operation. Many of the innovators in Business English are to be found in this group.

In-company

A great deal of training takes place on company premises with trainers either coming in from outside, or actually being employees of the company itself. The decision about whether to employ company language trainers is a political one, and there has in fact been a shift in the thinking of certain large companies over the past few years. Some companies which used to employ a large number of trainers now contract a great deal of their work out, either to local trainers or to trainers from Britain, the United States, and elsewhere.

Some companies and colleges have well-developed resource centres, with computers, language laboratories, video and audio systems, as well as books. Many training departments offer guided self-study opportunities for those who have no time to follow direct teaching. Employees or students may form their own 'study circles' or 'English clubs'.

Some implications

For the pre-experience learner

The learner is restricted in choice, and certainly constrained by the syllabus, the course, and the quality of support.

For the job-experienced learner

The learner's choice of institution will depend on what funds are available, and what is offered by the company. The choice will undoubtedly be affected by the power of advertising inside or outside the company, and by personal relationships and the experiences of colleagues who have previously attended courses at a particular place. He or she may be attracted to organizations with huge marketing budgets and very glossy literature. However, it may be difficult to get good advice.

For the training manager

Training managers and those responsible for sending company employees on language courses need to inform themselves of the choices available. The level of knowledge about what is available is much more sophisticated now than it used to be, but there is still a danger. Training departments can still be influenced by slick marketing, or a representative arriving at an opportune moment. The choices to be made—between individual tuition and group courses, between intensive and extensive courses, between in-house trainers and outside suppliers, between direct teaching and distance learning, between learning in the home country or in an English-speaking country such as the United Kingdom, the United States, or Australia (see Table 3.1 below), between the cheap and the more expensive—all need to be informed by a thorough appreciation of the needs of the learner, the cost-benefit ratio, and the nature of the supplier.

Table 3.1: Comparison between learning English in the home country and in an English-speaking country

Home	English-speaking country
Unavoidable mother tongue use	Full immersion
Closer to home, which may have practical advantages	Constant opportunities to meet native speakers
No 'authentic' need to use the target language	Genuine need to use the target language
No access to 'authentic' cultural setting	Constant exposure to language in context of the target culture
Job distractions, especially the telephone	No job distractions
Teacher the only model	Exposure to different accents/models
Less expensive	More expensive
These courses are often extensive, held for a few hours a week over several months. A disadvantage is that learners often drift and can become demotivated because of unclear objectives.	These courses are usually highly intensive.

4 RESOURCES

The Business English trainer

Background and experience

It is virtually impossible to describe a typical Business English trainer, as the profession has attracted people with widely differing backgrounds and experience. However, the following points will offer some common profiles.

Many Business English trainers will have had a university education, though not all. Some people come to the profession from a background in general TEFL teaching, and have a TEFL qualification. They may come to Business English by chance because they work in language schools which have decided to broaden the kinds of courses they offer to include Business English courses. On the other hand, they may be attracted to Business English and choose to make the change.

Why should TEFL teachers want to change to Business English? First, it provides a chance to work with highly-motivated learners who are often disciplined, intelligent, and dynamic. Second, it involves more than simply teaching language. In Business English, there are highly specific goals and objectives which demand a tight control of the course plan and careful selection of materials and activities. Third, Business English training may encompass professional skills as well as general language skills. These skills are taught in the context of a varied and fascinating subject matter. As a result, Business English provides a demanding and challenging field in which to develop a career.

Some Business English trainers come from a business background: they have worked in companies themselves and have useful knowledge of the way in which companies are organized and run. Some schools prefer to employ such people and feel that it is easier to train them in basic teaching skills than to train English teachers about business. These people may want more person-to-person contact than their previous jobs in industry could provide.

Still others may have started out with neither business nor TEFL teaching experience. They might originally have been geologists, architects, or school biology teachers, for example. Perhaps they fell into the profession by chance because personal circumstances led them to live abroad, so that teaching their mother tongue was a way to earn a living; and for them, teaching in a company was more interesting and lucrative than doing evening classes.

Whatever the background, it is important to stress that the Business English trainer is primarily a language teacher. He or she does not need to be an expert in any particular business. It is the learners who have the specific content knowledge and who are able to bring that knowledge to the classroom. Even when working with pre-experience learners, it is not the language trainer's role to teach the subject matter. Although it is of great value to be able to talk intelligently to learners about their work, it is of greater importance that the trainer should be seen as an expert in presenting and explaining the language, and in diagnosing the learners' language problems.

A good trainer will be able to work with an engineer, a product manager, or a foreign exchange dealer with equal skill and effectiveness, and the key to that effectiveness is being able to ask the right questions and make good use of the answers, whether they come from the learners themselves or from another source such as books or company documents. It is important to focus on the systems, procedures, and products that are at the centre of what the learner does in English, and to be able to deduce from this knowledge the language needs of each type of learner. The Business English trainer, therefore, needs to be informed about how language works. He or she will need to be able to identify the current language level of the learner and to select materials and set tasks that are appropriate in level as well as in content. Some trainers will also need to be able to set course objectives and devise course programmes, and to do this an in-depth knowledge of the language system in terms of skills, functions, structures, and vocabulary will be essential.

One type of experience which is very useful is to have lived abroad, to have learned at least one other language, and to have used it in real situations (not just in the classroom). This will foster an understanding of the feelings of inadequacy and insecurity experienced by language learners everywhere. It will also help to develop some of the personal skills outlined in the next section.

Personal skills

More important than qualifications and a background in business is the right balance of personal skills. This is the ingredient that is common to all good Business English trainers. What are these personal skills?

First, it is essential to have an outgoing personality, to like contact and interaction with a wide variety of people, and to be able to regard the less amiable learners as a challenge rather than a hindrance. The learner's agenda must come before the teacher's if the latter is to unlock the motivation and learning potential of each individual. Learners are quick to distinguish between the trainer who is sensitive to their real needs and the trainer who merely wants to pass the time as pleasantly as possible. While it is invaluable to have a good sense of humour, it is also vital that the trainer should be seen to be taking the course seriously.

A second skill is to be a good negotiator. Many job-experienced learners, particularly if they are managers, are used to dictating their own terms. However, a professional language trainer will know more about the best ways to teach a language than they do. It is important for the trainer to establish his or her credibility and professionalism so as to be able to discuss with the learners the best way to structure the course and agree the principles on which to work. This, in some cases, will require tact and diplomacy.

A third, vitally important skill is to be curious and interested in all aspects of business. One of the best ways for the trainer to 'unlock the learners' motivation and learning potential' is to show that he or she can relate to the subjects that most concern the learners. It will be much easier to do this if the trainer is genuinely fascinated by the way in which companies work: systems, organization, procedures, marketing strategies, financial planning, problem-solving, new technical developments, and products.

To summarize all these points: anyone thinking of Business English as a career need not be put off if they do not have all the right qualifications and background experience. These things can be gained with time. More important is to ask oneself:

– Do I really like people?
– Am I open-minded?
– Am I good at handling people?
– Am I genuinely interested in business topics?

Acquiring the resources

Skills

It is true in all walks of life that some people need to be trained, while others seem to be able to develop themselves through hard work, application, and experience. Taking courses is a way of speeding up the development process, and recognized qualifications are a prerequisite for some jobs.

Courses can also give confidence to people who previously had to rely on themselves: they may find encouragement from discovering that other people have similar problems and experiences, and they can get ideas for dealing with their own situation.

Many TEFL posts now require a recognized TEFL qualification, for example, the RSA/Cambridge Certificate or Diploma. The Cambridge Integrated TEFL Scheme (CITS) which is currently being developed will introduce a series of Advanced Diplomas, offering the opportunity to focus on special areas of interest in ELT. The first of these, the proposed Advanced Diploma in ELT Management, was due to have its first pilot scheme at the time of going to press. The RSA/Cambridge courses offer teachers the opportunity to develop their practical skills as well as to increase their prospects on the job market. The London Chamber of Commerce (LCCI) examinations board also offers the Diploma in Teaching English for Business (Dip TEB) and courses are run by the London Guildhall University which lead to this award. This examination is theoretical rather than practical.

For most Business English teaching posts, it is not necessary to have one of the more academic qualifications such as an MA in Applied Linguistics. (An exception to this rule might be jobs in universities or colleges of further education, teaching Business Studies or Economics students, especially in the Middle East.) Some universities and other organizations offer certificate and diploma courses in English for Specific Purposes, which involve about ten weeks rather than a full year of study.

Short courses and seminars specific to Business English are offered by several of the leading Business English schools and organizations, and whilst these do not lead to a qualification, they are usually of practical value.

Another way to develop skills is, of course, to get hands-on experience. People who have not worked in Business English before may find themselves in a situation where they are unable to get a job without experience but unable to get experience without a job. Probably the best kind of job to look for in this situation is one with a language school outside the

United Kingdom. Many language schools provide both general TEFL and in-company courses, and some will be willing to give training and help in getting into Business English. It is important to look for schools with a good reputation. In order to determine this, be ready to ask some searching questions at the interview. For example:

Which companies do you provide training for?

You should expect to hear the names of at least one or two larger companies. Big companies with a well-developed training policy are more likely to put their business with well-established schools who have a proven track record in providing efficient courses. The school should have a broad client base if you want to get experience in a variety of business fields.

How has the school developed in the last five years?

You should expect an answer which indicates that the school is aware of new developments in language training and is willing to adapt its courses accordingly. A school which is expanding in terms of the number and range of courses it runs will be more exciting to work for.

How many trainers are there? How many of these were here two years ago?

You may have your own preferences as to whether it is better to work for a large or a small organization. Large schools usually offer more security and better prospects for a career (for becoming a director of studies after a few years, for example). However, many small organizations have a good reputation for quality, and it can be very rewarding to work in a small but motivated team.

The turnover of staff is an important factor in both large and small organizations. If turnover is high, this can imply that working conditions are not satisfactory. It also means that experience cannot be passed on from older trainers to new ones, and therefore standards are likely to be lower.

Do you run courses in-company?

Courses which are run on-site in a company can provide the trainer with a more thorough knowledge of the way in which that company works. The trainer may have the chance to see its workers in action—for example, in the factory or in the computer room. It may be possible to set the learners practical, hands-on tasks such as showing someone around. This sort of experience is very valuable.

What kind of courses do you run in-company?

The answer may be either specific (tailor-made) or general Business English courses. Inexperienced Business English trainers will find it easier to work on general courses first. However, if you want to get a lot of experience, then a school which runs specific courses will be preferable.

Do you have your own in-house materials?

Schools which have developed their own materials show that they are more ready to design programmes and activities to suit the specific needs of their learners. However, be careful to check that teaching a particular course does not involve following the materials slavishly from the first page to the last. In-house materials that can be used selectively, perhaps on a modular basis, will give the trainer more opportunity to respond to the needs of individual learners. The selection process will involve more effort and uncertainty initially, but will be much more rewarding in the end.

Do your trainers develop their own materials?

You may or may not feel that you want to get involved in materials development yourself. However, if other trainers in the same institutions are doing so, it will be an indication that the school encourages teacher development and creativity as well as recognizing that this is often a good way to cater for learners with highly specific needs. Be careful to check, however, that it does not imply that no other materials exist within the school. If you are going to be required to develop materials, make sure the school provides time for this within the normal working day.

What assistance or guidance do you give to new trainers?

If you are relatively inexperienced, then it will be important to work for a school that will be supportive. At the start of your contract, you should expect either an induction course lasting one or two weeks, or a probationary period where you will be working with a more experienced trainer who can give you the help and support you need.

Do you arrange further training for your teachers?

Trainers who want to develop their career after a few years may need to acquire new skills such as how to design courses, how to write materials, or how to run special skills courses (for example, in negotiating). Even very experienced trainers need new ideas to stimulate and refresh their approach. A school with high standards will recognize this need and should make some provision for its trainers to attend courses. Some schools may run courses in-house, others may bring in outside consultants or offer to pay course fees at another institution.

Do your trainers belong to teachers' associations or go to conferences?

Teachers' associations such as TESOL and IATEFL can offer a lot of support to their members in the form of newsletters (which contain useful articles and ideas), conferences, and seminars. Schools which encourage their teachers to join associations, and which provide financial support to attend conferences, will ensure that their teaching staff are up-to-date with developments in the profession. Conferences provide a forum for trainers to meet others working in the same field, to exchange ideas and opinions, and to learn new techniques. They can be stimulating and refreshing, and provide a foundation for networking, both nationally and internationally.

Finally, in order to develop personal skills as well as gaining professional experience, it is invaluable for native speakers to spend at least a couple of years teaching abroad. This, combined with working in a big company, will provide a good foundation for a career in Business English.

Knowledge

As we have stressed before, it is a misconception that in the field of ESP the trainer needs to be an expert in the subject matter. He or she is not teaching business strategies, nor good management practice, nor economic theory. If the learners need to know about these things (as is sometimes the case with pre-experienced learners) they will learn them from other sources. The language trainer's task is to train businesspeople to communicate in English about the subjects they are specialized in. An exception to this can be found in the former communist states of Eastern Europe, and the former Soviet Union. Here the capitalist systems and procedures involved in marketing, banking, and finance may be very new to some learners, even if they are job-experienced. Some language trainers in these countries may therefore find themselves having to teach the theory and practice of business as well as the language.

As mentioned when discussing personal skills, it is important to be able to relate to the learners and their needs and this is easier if the trainer understands what their jobs involve. Reaching a good understanding of the job means: first, being able to ask intelligent questions; and second, being able to fit the new information into a familiar pattern.

What can a prospective trainer do to inform him or herself and to build up confidence in dealing with specialists?

The first option is to read relevant material. This might include some textbooks: for example, the kinds of books used on Business Studies courses, MBA courses, or commercial and vocational courses. (A basic list is given in the Suggestions for Further Reading.) Other appropriate reading might be recommended by experienced colleagues or language schools. For those working in a college or university, it will be important to find out what textbooks the students use on their special subject courses. It will not always be necessary to read the whole book, only to understand some of the basic concepts and viewpoints. For those working in-company, it could be useful to ask the learners themselves what they have read that relates to their work.

Magazines, journals, newspapers, and other kinds of literature are also important, and have the value of being more up-to-date and less theoretical than books. Dip into the *Financial Times* or *The Economist*, skim through the business pages of the national daily newspapers. Especially useful are articles on new developments in different fields of industry. For instance, if the learners work for a car manufacturing company, then news items on new models, in-car computers, traffic management, or buying trends are likely to provide useful topics for the classroom.

As already noted in Chapter 1, Business English (like other varieties of ESP) involves a certain amount of specific terminology, and this is often frightening at first. Reading articles and books helps the new trainer to become familiar with some of the terminology and special expressions used in Business English. It will also be helpful to buy a Business English dictionary. (See Suggestions for Further Reading for a list.) If a learner asks a question about a specialized term which the trainer does not know, the first thing he or she can do is to check the available dictionaries. (Note that it is better for a trainer to be honest if there is a term he or she does not know: the trainer should not expect to be an expert, and the learner should not expect it either.) If the term is so specialized that it is not included in a specialist dictionary, then the learner should be advised to check with someone in his or her company who might know the meaning. There may be people in the same department who speak good English and know a lot of the jargon of the job; alternatively, there may be someone at head office, or in an English or American subsidiary who can help. Some companies may have glossaries for technical words common to their field. The important thing is not to panic if there are some strange or difficult words: the trainer's role is to help the learner acquire knowledge, not to provide all the answers.

In-company trainers should make sure that they are well-informed about the company where they work: that means reading the company literature such as brochures, annual reports, and product information. Even if they work in a language school and deal with a number of different companies, it is still useful to know something about each of them.

In addition to printed material, TV and video material can be useful. Watching business programmes and documentaries can extend a trainer's general knowledge and understanding of business topics and concerns. Even those who do not live in an English-speaking country can buy (or persuade their employers to buy) some programmes on video. (Addresses to write to are given in the Appendix.) A number of training videos have been produced which are used by companies to train their staff in basic skills such as using the telephone, running meetings, giving presentations, and so on. These can be a useful way to gain knowledge about good business practices and to see in action the kinds of skills the learners need to develop in English.

One important way to learn about business is through working with knowledgeable Business English learners, especially job-experienced learners. The teacher can often gain more insight into the workings of companies through asking questions and listening to the answers, than through books. Accessing these human resources is one of the skills that is vital in becoming a good Business English trainer.

5 PERFORMANCE OBJECTIVES FOR BUSINESS ENGLISH

The need to emphasize performance

As already stated, one of the main characteristics of Business English is the emphasis on performance—training learners to become operationally effective. For people in business, the priority is to be able to understand and get their message across, and for the majority of Business English learners many of the refinements of language are quite simply not relevant. For people in full-time jobs, time is often severely constrained, and acquiring knowledge for its own sake (though it may be pleasurable for some) is out of the question.

What the majority of business learners need to acquire could be broadly summarized as follows:

– confidence and fluency in speaking
– skills for organizing and structuring information
– sufficient language accuracy to be able to communicate ideas without ambiguity and without stress for the listener
– strategies for following the main points of fast, complex, and imperfect speech
– strategies for clarifying and checking unclear information
– speed of reaction to the utterances of others
– clear pronunciation and delivery
– an awareness of appropriate language and behaviour for the cultures and situations in which they will operate.

Some learners may also need to develop practical reading and writing skills.

In Business English, these performance criteria need to be seen in the context of specific business situations which the learner will be involved in. If the requirements of a typical job are analysed, it can be seen, for example, that a learner has to attend meetings which are carried out in English and that he or she has to follow what is going on and be able to make a contribution. The learner may also have to make telephone calls in English and

Table 5.1: Business skills checklist

Speaking
Giving a formal presentation
Giving an informal presentation
Instructing or demonstrating on the job
Giving descriptions and explanations

Interacting
Visiting a company or receiving visitors
Showing visitors around or being shown around
Entertaining or being entertained

Participating in discussions and informal meetings
Participating in formal meetings
Chairing meetings
Interviewing
Negotiating

Telephoning

Listening
Following presentations, lectures, or talks
Following instructions
Following descriptions and explanations
Following training sessions

Reading

Documents	*Skills*
Telexes	Reading for detail
Letters and faxes	
Memos and short reports	
Professional journals	Reading quickly for general
Textbooks	information
Long reports	Scanning for specific points
Contracts and legal documents	
Technical specifications and manuals	

Writing
Telexes
Letters and faxes
Memos and short reports
Long reports and articles for professional journals
Editing the letters or reports of others

send and receive faxes written in English. If the learner sometimes meets business associates from other countries, then a certain amount of socializing will also be important. A list of the essential language skills needed to do all these aspects of the job successfully can be drawn up, and will provide a basis for the course that the learner in the example will follow. A checklist of business skills is given in Table 5.1.

Analysing the specific needs of an individual learner and defining the skills objectives of that learner is the subject of Chapter 8 in Part Two. This chapter explains some of the implications of skills training for the prospective Business English trainer, and how it affects what happens in the classroom.

Skills training: basic principles

If priority is given to developing the kinds of skills listed above, what does this mean for the role of the language trainer? What kinds of classroom behaviours will be encouraged and what activities will be used to stimulate these behaviours?

The communicative approach

The first step is to create a classroom environment in which real communication can take place and can be practised continuously. This will involve a number of strategies. It will mean that all the personal skills set out on page 27 will be important: if the trainer is an open and approachable person, it is more likely that the learners will feel confident and relaxed. In this frame of mind, they will be more likely to speak, and speaking will develop their fluency. Interaction can also be encouraged by not over-correcting (drawing attention to every tiny mistake discourages people from speaking and also breaks up the flow of communication), by asking plenty of questions, and by giving people time to answer (interruptions also discourage the more diffident learners). In other words, the main principles of the communicative approach apply to Business English as much as to General English.

Part of the equation is creating good group dynamics. Members of a group should not feel exposed to criticism from the others, but rather that they are all facing a common problem together. If they are able to laugh, with the others, at difficulties which they have in common, this will help enormously. Activities should be seen as a chance to practise and develop skills in a pleasurable way, not as frightening tests of ability. Business-people are by nature competitive and most will respond well to a challenge, but tasks should be set at the right level so that they are within the scope of the learner.

It is important that the learners should not feel embarrassed if they do not know something, or do not understand. They should be encouraged to treat the trainer as a resource: to be open about their problems and to ask for help rather than surreptitiously flipping through a pocket dictionary. When they ask questions, learners are practising the vital skills of checking and clarifying information—skills they will frequently need in real business situations.

Learner involvement in course design

At the beginning of a course, it is important to discuss with the learners the course objectives and methods for achieving these objectives. It is valuable to explain the goals of each lesson, and the reason why certain types of activities and materials have been chosen. It will not be possible to discuss the details of activities and materials at the start of a course because the options available will not be clear; but as the course progresses, the learners can play a gradually stronger role in deciding how to spend their class time.

Input v. output

Most important in Business English training is deciding on the balance of training time to be spent on input (introducing or recycling target language) and output (providing opportunities for practice and skills development).

If a lot of time is spent on introducing long lists of words or expressions, on carefully explaining the finer details of a grammar point, or on the detailed reading in class of lengthy written texts, then clearly the time left for practising speaking will be much reduced. By carefully selecting the language that a particular learner, or group of learners, needs, the trainer will be able to reduce significantly the amount of time needed for formal input. Able learners who want to extend their vocabulary and grammar significantly can be given material to study in their own time rather than wasting valuable class time focusing on the printed page.

The question of what target language to select and how to select it is the subject of Chapter 9 in Part Two; however, it is important to stress here that the amount of course time needed for input will be a small fraction of the whole. A much larger proportion of the course time will be needed for output. If the aim is to develop fluency and faster reactions, then the need for practice time will be greater.

Task-based learning

The kind of practice the learner gets is also important. The basic fabric of a Business English course should be tasks which simulate those of the learner's real situation as closely as possible. These tasks must have specific objectives which can be clearly defined at the outset, and which relate to the learner's overall objectives in following the course as well as to his or her level of ability.

Practice tasks may be long or short. They may include, for example: asking a learner to describe one of his or her company's products or to compare two different products; asking two group members to imagine they are business associates meeting for the first time; setting up a telephone role play or a simulated meeting; getting the learner to prepare a short presentation defending a certain point of view. These are very broad descriptions of the kinds of tasks that can be set. In the classroom, the task will be much more closely defined so that the learners know exactly what the setting is, who they are supposed to be, what sort of things they are supposed to communicate, and what is expected of them in performance terms. Setting up the task thoroughly is essential in order to get maximum value from it—much time can be wasted if learners do not know what they are supposed to be doing. The selection of appropriate tasks will depend on the needs of the learners in relation to their jobs—i.e. what business situations they have to deal with. In the case of pre-experience learners, the tasks will need to refer more to support material (such as texts or video), and will rely on only minimal input from the learners.

Feedback

It is also essential that learners should get helpful and constructive feedback on their performance, and this means relating the task to the performance objectives. It may be interesting for the learners to know that they made mistakes in the verb tenses, but they must also know whether these mistakes actually affected the success or failure of the task. In other words, the feedback should be, first and foremost, on the task as a whole. Did they communicate effectively? Were they easy to understand? Did they manage to clarify misunderstandings? Did they use appropriate politeness forms? Only after that feedback has been given is it valuable to draw attention to specific language errors that may have contributed to lack of overall clarity or precision.

PART TWO

Analysing the needs of the learners

6 DESCRIBING LEVELS OF PERFORMANCE

In Chapter 5, the need to emphasize skills training was explained, and a list was given of some very broad-based statements of performance criteria which are important to the majority of Business English learners. The first of these was fluency in speaking. If a concept such as fluency is taken as an objective for a course, several difficulties immediately arise. How is fluency to be defined? How can degrees of fluency be measured? If degrees of fluency cannot be measured, how is it possible to establish whether progress has been made? These, and similar questions about other performance areas, have to be answered and more precise definitions of learning objectives have to be reached.

Who needs to define levels of performance and why?

First of all, the training organization needs to be able to see what level of ability the learner has at the start of a course: this is important for forming homogeneous groups (if the learner is going to learn in a group) and for determining the content and substance of the course. Taking into account the time available, the training organization will want to set goals for the learner(s) that can be realistically achieved. This can only be done if the starting level is clearly established.

Similarly, at the end of a course, the training organization will want to be able to show that the training was effective. Thus the exit level of each learner needs to be demonstrated in some way. A training organization can easily develop its own entry and exit tests which it can use to differentiate the types of learners who commonly attend its courses.

However, it is not only the training organization which has an interest in knowing the levels of ability of course participants. If the training is being paid for by a sponsoring organization (for example, the company, in the case of job-experienced learners), then it is obviously of some importance to the sponsors to know that their money has not been wasted. They will want the results of training to be clearly demonstrated. The training organization cannot comply with this need by passing on a test result such as '8 out of 10', or 'B+'. Such scores are meaningless unless they can be related to norms for the population at large.

In addition, the learners themselves need to know what their capabilities are. If they are going to be using English in an international context, they will want to know how their English compares to that of non-native users worldwide. How will others see them? Will they give the impression of being accomplished speakers, or will they appear stupid? How much and how long will they need to study to reach an 'acceptable' level? (What is an acceptable level?)

These problems can only be solved by setting up a performance scale which can be used to evaluate all Business English learners worldwide according to common criteria. Such a scale must distinguish levels of ability in each of the key skills areas. It must define what tasks a learner can or cannot do at each level, and with what degree of success a learner can be expected to carry out the task.

Performance scales

The first ever performance scale was the Stages of Attainment Scale developed in 1976 by ELTDU (the English Language Teaching Development Unit—then an affiliate of Oxford University Press). This scale was developed in response to the requirement of a large Swedish company, SKF, to be able to assess the level of English needed to carry out certain jobs and the amount of language training needed by the people in those jobs in order to reach the required level. It is a complex document comprising no fewer than 27 business skills areas, including, for example, Listening/Speaking: dealing with visitors, use of the telephone, verbally relaying information; Reading and Writing: routine/non-routine correspondence, journals, PR/press, reports etc. In each of the skills areas, there are definitions of what learners should be able to do at each of eight levels of attainment (A/B = Elementary; C/D = Threshold level; G/H = Near-native competence). Although the definitions of ability relate to performance, the scale is closely tied into a set of language specifications which detail the grammatical and lexical knowledge which a learner is expected to have at each level.

Since the publication of the ELTDU Scale, a number of other scales have been developed, and the idea has been greatly refined and simplified for

easier access to users. Most scales now only offer definitions of performance in four or five main skills areas (Speaking, Speaking and Listening,
Listening, Reading and Writing), and the number of levels distinguished
may be only five or six. This makes it easier and faster to assess the
learner's level—an important consideration for businesspeople with a
heavy workload.

Nowadays, organizations such as the British Council, large company
training departments, and the leading language schools have developed
their own scales to comply with their own requirements. This means that
there are a number of different scales in use around the world, and it can
be confusing to try to compare them. In the field of General English, the
examining bodies such as Cambridge and RSA have got together to work
out a universal system for testing and assessment. However, in Business
English, definitions of performance objectives and methods of assessment
still vary greatly from one organization to another.

Below are some extracts from three scales: the ELTDU Stages of
Attainment Scale (an eight-point scale) which has already been mentioned
above; the English Speaking Union (ESU) Scale, which is a nine-level
scale, widely used in determining general language ability, and not
specifically adapted to Business English; and a scale developed in-house by
the Finnish company United Paper Mills (UPM) (eight points), as an
example of a scale designed for use with business and professional people
which can be readily used by both language training professionals and
company training managers with little knowledge of language learning.

ELTDU Scale: dealing with visitors, Level B

Can welcome visitors and perform introductions, giving a brief outline of personal details, purpose of visit etc. Can give a simple
description of work in hand. But cannot "talk shop" or make social
chat, or answer unpredictable questions.

ESU Scale, Level 2

Uses a narrow range of language, adequate for basic needs and
simple situations. Does not really have sufficient language to cope
with normal day-to-day, real-life communication, but basic communication is possible with adequate opportunities for assistance. Uses
short, often inaccurately and inappropriately worded messages, with
constant lapses in fluency.

UPM Language Ability Scale, Level 2: Extremely limited communication

Some everyday vocabulary and phrases are known, e.g. normal greetings, perhaps also some words connected with own subject sphere.

A person at this level can "survive" in the language (e.g. travel without getting lost, give basic details about himself) but cannot function in it in his work.

ELTDU Stages of Attainment Scale, external business meetings and negotiations, Level F

Can take part in negotiations. Can argue for and against a case effectively. Has sufficient range of language to talk about most spheres of the business. But is still unaware of the nuances of meaning conveyed by intonation and careful choice of words.

ESU Scale, Level 6

Uses the language with confidence in all but the most demanding situations. Noticeable lapses in accuracy, fluency, appropriacy and organization, but communication and comprehension are effective on most occasions, and are easily restored when difficulties arise.

UPM Language Ability Scale, Level 6: Good communicative ability

Has full command of the grammatical structures of the language; begins to use nuances of meaning successfully; has a rather extensive general vocabulary.

At this level a person is able to take part in discussions and negotiations in the role, for instance, of seller.

Testing and assessment

Just as it is difficult to define language attainment in performance terms, so it is also difficult to measure that attainment. It is simpler by far to assess the learner's knowledge of grammar by setting a multiple choice, itemized test of the traditional type. But does knowledge of grammar have any bearing on the learner's ability to understand and communicate orally? Unfortunately, there are many cases where there is a mismatch: some learners have had a thorough grounding in grammar at school, but have never had to use the language and have a low level of communicative ability; others, who may have acquired English on the job or while travelling, may have very poor grammatical knowledge but a reasonable ability to communicate.

If the objective of a course is to improve effective communication, then a different type of assessment is needed. However, the assessment of oral communication skills—usually by giving an oral test—is by its very nature subjective. There are two ways of overcoming this problem. The first is to set up the oral test in such a way that the subjective element is minimized. This means that strict guidelines for the test have to be laid down: the kinds of questions to be asked and the kinds of tasks to be set must be specified and structured according to difficulty. Here, the definitions of expected performance at different levels are essential for evaluation. But the tester must be very familiar with the scale being used, and a lot of experience is needed to distinguish different levels of ability in accordance with the definitions.

The second method is to combine the oral test with objective tests such as reading comprehension, listening comprehension, and possibly a grammar test. By combining scores on different types of test, an overall and perhaps fairer picture can emerge.

Published tests and examinations

There are now three British examining bodies offering examinations leading to certification in Business English. These are the London Chamber of Commerce and Industry Examinations Board (which offers the oral examination Spoken English for Industry and Commerce, as well as the written English for Business examination; the University of Cambridge Examinations Syndicate (which offers the Certificate in English for International Business and Trade, an examination targeted at secretaries and administrative personnel); and the University of Oxford Delegacy of Examinations (which offers the Oxford International Business English Certificate, targeted more at those people in the company who have executive responsibilities). Business students sometimes take General English examinations such as the Cambridge First Certificate or Proficiency, or the American-based TOEFL and TOEIC. The last-mentioned is particularly popular in Japan and has a business component.

Individual countries may have their own examinations. Many European Chambers of Commerce set examinations—for example, the Franco-British Chamber of Commerce in France and the British Chamber of Commerce in Milan.

In addition to these examinations, there are some published tests available which are designed to show the learner's level of attainment on a particular scale. The ELTDU Scale mentioned on page 44 was accompanied by a test battery which placed prospective learners on the eight-point scale in each of the four main language skills. Similarly, some other commercially available scales, such as the LTS scale, are also used in conjunction with a placement test. (For information about scales and tests which can be purchased, see the Appendix.)

Carrying out assessment yourself

A trainer working for an organization that has its own system of testing and assessment will clearly follow the guidelines and procedures laid down. However, if the organization has no system, or if the trainer is working independently, then it will be important to find a workable system. The trainer will need to determine the entry and exit levels of the learners, and to set precise course objectives. Ideally, such a trainer will need to get hold of a scale and become very familiar with it.

A trainer who is not used to assessing level will need to build up a bank of cases to refer to. It will be useful to start a collection of samples of work carried out by different learners. These may be examples of written work (for example, letters or reports that learners have written without help) or tape recordings of interviews, presentations, or role-plays. By analysing these samples and comparing them, it will be possible to see more clearly how they match the performance definitions in the scale being used. When the trainer feels confident that he or she has found a 'typical level 3' or a 'typical level 5', the samples can be kept for reference in the future.

Some transcripts of learner output are included below, with comments that attempt to show some of the key features that will be critical for making assessments.

As it is relatively easy to distinguish between beginners/elementary learners at one end of the scale, and very advanced learners at the other end, these extracts focus on the grey areas in the middle bands. Each extract is accompanied by comments on spoken performance with regard to these main parameters: size of utterance (i.e. ability to maintain communication in English over long periods); speed (compared to normal native speaker speed); fluency (or lack of hesitancy); comprehensibility (with reference to accuracy, control, and organization of the message, and pronunciation/ stress); complexity (ability to handle the details of a topic); flexibility (ability to change topic and to keep in touch with the interlocutor in terms of emphasis and interest); independence (degree to which the speaker needs help or tolerance from the audience); mother tongue interference (use of non-English words or sentence structures); range of vocabulary (does the speaker have enough vocabulary to express the full depth of meaning that he or she wishes to convey?); appropriacy (appropriate selection of expression or vocabulary according to the situation); and accuracy (rate of errors in grammar or vocabulary). (Note: T = trainer, L = learner.)

Speaker 1

The first extract is from a presentation given by a product manager responsible for cosmetic products.

Anyway the profit before tax is six per cent—that's not too bad, so we still can live with it—but we have to do something—er—with this branch—to bring it up, to equalize, to bring to a reasonable level. And that's what I want to tell you in the second part: what we will do with the marketing mix—er—factors.

As you know, we have four marketing mix instruments: there is— er—distribution; there is the price instrument, there is the instru- ment—er—which that's communication, advertising; and the fourth instrument is the product [pronounced /'prəʊdʌkt/]—er—product [pronounced /prɒdʌkt/] itself. The product itself is the main instru- ment.

Let us start with the distribution instrument and—er—if we see the Market Audits summary distribution study—er—it is made, which is made, we see that—er—the most important outlets are the chemists and the others. Why are they the most most important out- lets? Because we have the biggest market share for these outlets and they are just—there are just a few of them we have to deal with. So we should concentrate in future on the chemists and on the five others—er—to make our business. The grocery outlets have— shouldn't be forgotten, but they are second priority.

Let me come to the second point. The price policy.

We have, nowadays, we have a price which is at about 20p. You know—as you know, the price range in the market is between 5 and 25p, we we are still in the upper third of the price range and in qual- ity we are also in the upper third so we shouldn't do anything with the price at the moment. We should keep it constantly.

Commentary

Size The speaker can handle long periods of monologue. (This is just a short extract from a 15-minute presentation.)

Speed He speaks at normal speed.

Fluency There are a few hesitations and false starts, but these are not unduly distracting.

Comprehensibility His message is mainly clear, although some points could probably be expressed more precisely (for example, the point about the chemists and the others); while it is not evident here, his pronunci- ation and stress patterns were close to standard and easy to listen to. His message is well-organized and each new point is clearly signalled.

Independence He needs no help and only a little tolerance from his audi- ence.

Mother tongue interference (German) One or two sentences are not very English (for example, 'They are just . . . a few of them we have to deal with.').

Range of vocabulary In general, he has no problems with vocabulary in this extract, apart from hesitancy over 'communication—advertising'.

Appropriacy The language is appropriate for the situation.

Accuracy Generally good. (One mistake in tense: 'the study which is made'; one with use of the adverb 'constantly'.)

This short sample cannot demonstrate the overall flexibility of the speaker, nor listening and interactive skills, although these are also factors that should be taken into consideration in assessing level.

In short, it can be seen that this is a competent speaker, who, if attending an English course, would mainly need to work on refining his skills: he could further extend his ability to express ideas precisely, and could work on increasing his range, fluency, and accuracy.

Speaker 2

This speaker is a loss prevention engineer working in an insurance company. His job is to inspect commercial properties and advise on risks: sometimes the properties are in the United Kingdom. In this extract, he simulates a presentation to a client company on the subject of fire risk. (T=Trainer, L=Learner)

L   In this step there are two rooms which are exposed to fire—they are naturally exposed to fire. You have the coffee room—because it's allowed it's allowed to smoke in this room. And you have the boiler room and—er—these two rooms have not any smoke detector. They haven't smoke detectors so—er—it will be a good idea to add a detector to install a detector in each of these rooms. I think it very important because these two rooms are very sensitive points and they are not equipped with smoke detectors. An automatic fire detection system is efficient if—if its alarms are immediately followed by—by—by an intervention— a fireman or somebody in the estate, in the premises. But—er— if it's—if it is a case during the day there is always somebody there. During the night, nobody can treat—can er—can do an intervention after an alarm very quickly, so it will be a good idea, it's a good idea to—er—to report to report the alarms— er—until a place where there is always somebody with a tele- phone transmitter, an automatic telephone transmitter.

T   Is that easy to do?

L Yes. Yes, it's easy to do. Or perhaps you have special companies. In France we call these—er—*télésurveillances.* They—er—it's a company which is connected with all the fire detection alarm systems. And when there is an alarm in the company, they make an intervention directly—or they can call the firemen.

Commentary

Size He is able to maintain long interactions and monologues.

Speed Normal.

Fluency Quite a lot of hesitancy, repetition of words, and false starts to sentences.

Comprehensibility He gets the message across, but there is some repetition and circumlocution. His pronunciation is typical for a French speaker, but he is reasonably easy to understand. He could organize his ideas more efficiently—(for example, the first point is that the company needs to install smoke detectors; the second point is that they should connect the detectors by telephone to a surveillance company).

Independence He is able to function fairly independently, although a listener without knowledge of French might need to clarify some details.

Mother tongue interference (French) Some words ('intervention') and sentence structure ('it's allowed to smoke') are direct translations from French.

Range of vocabulary Although he knows most of the job-related vocabulary he needs, he sometimes has to talk around an idea because he cannot find the right words (for example, *télésurveillance*).

Appropriacy He could make the recommendations more strongly (for example, 'You really need to install smoke detectors' or 'You should consider installing smoke detectors' rather than 'It will be a good idea . . .').

Accuracy He is mainly accurate although there are a few mistakes (for example, 'in this step', meaning 'on this floor'; 'until a place', meaning 'to a place').

Flexibility and interactive skills cannot be demonstrated here.

In summary, we can see that this speaker has good ability and good strategies for communicating the main ideas, but still needs to improve the fluency and organization of the message. He could work at increasing the accuracy of his structure and vocabulary, and could also be made more aware of the appropriacy of different kinds of language.

Speaker 3

This learner is of Turkish origin but now lives in Germany. In this extract, he role-plays a telephone conversation with his trainer in which he practises giving directions.

L How are you? It is nice to hear your voice. I never heard it.

T That's right. We have written a lot of letters but never spoken. So how are you enjoying your stay in England?

L Oh I am very glad. Yes. But only a problem with English weather.

T You're feeling cold?

L Yes. But I take enough pullover—no problem at the moment. [pause]

T I got your message, and you suggested meeting this evening.

L Oh yeah.

T You are in Bath, is that right?

L Yes, it is okay.

T I'm in Poole, as you know. So I don't in fact know Bath. Maybe you can give me some directions and make some suggestions about where we could meet?

L Yes. I have been with my colleague in a small pub in the city. It was very nice. I recommend you to meet—er—Green Tree.

T Sorry. I didn't catch that. What's the name?

L Green Tree. The name of the pub—stay in Green Street.

T Could you give me some idea where that is? I'm coming by train so I'd be walking up from the station. Is it far?

L It is not far. You go straight direction city and then—er—you see—er—the big church.

T Is this Bath Abbey? Do you mean the Abbey?

L I think the name of the church is Sankt Paul. In the near is a big shopping centre. The name of the building is Waitstore of the right hand. And then you go the first left street. And then you see on the left side 'Green Tree'.

Commentary

Size The learner's responses are generally short, with little elaboration.

Speed Fairly normal.

Fluency He speaks quite fluently, with not much hesitation.

Comprehensibility His directions are not very clear. His pronunciation is sometimes difficult to understand, and his mistakes could cause confusion. He does not check if the listener has followed correctly, and does not help the listener enough. (For example, when answering the question 'Do you mean Bath Abbey?', he does not say categorically 'No'.)

Independence He is not a very independent speaker. The trainer needs to prompt and clarify quite frequently to keep the interaction moving and to get the right information.

Interference It is interesting that this speaker shows interference from German, which he knows better than English.

Range of vocabulary He has all the words he needs in this conversation.

Appropriacy His use of social language is appropriate, although he would need to say more in order to sound more friendly.

Accuracy He makes a number of mistakes in both structure and vocabulary.

Listening and interactive skills He seemed to misunderstand the question 'You are in Bath, is that right?'—his response would be more appropriate for the question 'Can we meet in Bath?' Apart from this, he understood and responded well. However, the trainer supported him by speaking clearly.

In summary, we can see that this learner still has quite a long way to go to increase his overall communicative effectiveness. He is likely to be rated as lower in ability than he actually is because of poor pronunciation and accuracy. He needs to work on these areas, and to practise exchanging information and clarifying. He also needs to extend his interactive and social skills.

The training gap

The training gap can be defined as the difference between the starting level and target level of a learner or group of learners. The training gap is arrived at by establishing the starting level (through testing or interviewing), and by carrying out needs analysis. It can be expressed in terms of performance by reference to one or other of the accredited performance scales.

The training gap in no way relates to any absolute lack of ability. Nor are the objectives set at the highest level of the performance scale. The gap relates only to the difference between current level and the target level as defined by the job needs. The training gap may not be uniform across the different language skills. A salesperson may need to speak and listen at a good level, but not require more than an intermediate level in reading and writing. Nor will the gap be uniform within a skills area. For example, a senior executive may measure high on the scale in spoken skills when tested within a context where he or she is in control, and where the subject matter is familiar. In this situation, the trainer might assume that the learner's needs are minimal. However, when put in a situation where the learner is not in control or has to deal with unfamiliar subject matter, he or she may show a much lower level of ability. If the needs analysis indicates that the learner must achieve competence in this second type of situation, then a training gap appears. Thus the training gap highlights what should be the focus of training. If asked to define the training gap at the start of a course, the trainer would expect to say, for example: 'This learner is good at communicating in situation X, but finds situation Y complex and difficult.'

The training gap refers to what needs to be achieved in the long term rather than what can be achieved on a particular course. Thus it is not the same as the objectives for the course, although it will be important in setting priorities.

The trainer may well be asked to estimate how long (in terms of hours of tuition) the learner needs to achieve a target level. This is difficult to assess accurately since learners of different ability progress at different rates, and some may have more motivation, or more time and more opportunities to practise than others. Table 6.1, drawn up by Brendan Carroll and Patrick Hall for their book *Make your own Language Tests* (see the Suggestions for Further Reading), gives the average number of hours required to progress from one level to another on an eight-point scale. As can be seen, it takes proportionately much longer to progress from one level to the next at an advanced stage than it does to progress from one level to the next at an early stage.

Table 6.1: Estimate of progress in tuition hours

Present performance levels	2	3	4	5	6	7	8
2	•	90	190	340	540	820	1170
3		•	100	250	450	730	1080
4			•	150	350	630	980
5				•	200	480	830
6					•	280	630
7						•	350

e.g.
from 4 to 7 = 630 hrs
from 2 to 6 = 540 hrs

Intended target levels: 2 3 4 5 6 7 8

Progress estimates:

Bands	hours		Bands	hours
2–3	= 90 hrs		5–6	= 200 hrs
3–4	= 100 hrs		6–7	= 280 hrs
4–5	= 150 hrs		7–8	= 350 hrs

The training gap is a valuable term of reference for both the learner and the trainer when considering what is achievable and what is possible. It is also very important for training managers and for the people who set up training programmes for companies or for educational establishments, because it provides the means for evaluating training in the short term and for setting the results of training in the context of long-term objectives. The definition of the training gap provides the means for making those involved in the training more accountable.

7 JOB ANALYSIS

The first step in identifying the learners and finding out what needs they are likely to have is to look at the kind of jobs they are doing. Even if the learners have not started their jobs yet, it will be possible to see what general category they are going to fit into, and thus to predict what kinds of needs they will have in the future and what will be useful to include in their course.

Below, we set out the main categories of jobs together with some notes on how the training may be shaped according to these categories. We would like to stress, however, that being able to make some predictions about needs on the basis of the job description does not preclude the requirement for carrying out a full needs analysis as described in Chapter 8. There are a great many people whose jobs and needs do not fit neatly into categories. This outline is to help build up a general pattern of understanding about business and what businesspeople do, and it will lay the foundations for needs analysis and language analysis and the selection of course components.

Job categories

In the next three sections, we draw distinctions between three very broad categories: (1) managerial, (2) technical, and (3) secretarial/clerical positions.

Managers as learners

A large proportion of those who seek language training because of the demands of their job are managers. This is because it is mainly managers who work with international affairs and who therefore travel most and deal most with people from other countries in face-to-face situations. Also, as they are near the top of the pay scale, their companies are usually more willing to spend money on training them.

Senior managers

Senior managers, in particular, are likely to ask for, and be given, individual tuition. They have tight schedules and severe time constraints, and they will not want to waste time by having to fit in with other people's needs and programmes. They will want their course to be as specific and as relevant to their own needs as possible.

Since they have to meet with important people from outside the company, they will want to give the best possible impression of competence and authority and will require advanced language skills with a high degree of refinement in terms of accuracy and appropriacy.

In terms of job skills (see the list in Chapter 5), senior managers will probably need: chairing meetings, participating in meetings, negotiating, giving formal presentations, and socializing—especially entertaining.

As they are involved with the running of the company as a whole, senior managers will want to discuss global concepts such as the principles of management, the organization of the company and its rationale, decision-making procedures, long-term planning, and defining the company image. They will also probably have special areas of responsibility such as finance, human resources, or marketing.

Used to being in control and making decisions, senior managers will probably take an assertive role in their own training. Most will be confident but if they feel that their language skills are relatively poor, they may be somewhat sensitive and embarrassed on this point. As intelligent people, they will not wish to be talked down to, given activities which seem facile, or given materials that lack credibility. The approach that will

work best with most senior managers is to enable them to demonstrate their expertise by giving them the opportunity to explain what happens in their company, to express their own ideas, and to discuss problems at a high conceptual level. They will want to be challenged by tasks which are demanding and require imagination. They will also want to be given feedback on the language they are using and the overall impression they are creating when using English.

Senior managers are used to concentrating intensively for long hours and they will expect their English language trainers to do the same. Working with people at this level can therefore be very demanding, but also very rewarding.

Middle and junior managers

Many of the comments on senior managers, above, apply also to middle and junior managers, who may after all be the same people at an earlier stage of their careers. There are, however, some differences.

Middle and junior managers may be offered individual tuition or may join group courses of one kind or another. If the latter is the case, then they will get a more general business training with less emphasis on their own specific situation. On the other hand, many of them enjoy being in a group because of the opportunities for lively discussions, role-plays, and simulations. They will probably need less refinement than managers at a senior level, although this will vary according to the actual job they do.

In terms of skills, middle and junior managers will also need meetings skills but are less likely to need to chair meetings. They will need presentation skills, but may not need to make very formal presentations. They are more likely to need telephoning and report-writing skills as they will probably not have support from highly qualified executive secretaries. When dealing with people from outside the company, they will probably be more informal. Other skills requirements will depend on the job.

Middle and junior managers work within a more closely defined area than senior managers: they are not concerned with the running of the company as a whole, but with a particular department or product area. They will normally deal with very practical everyday matters such as procedures for dealing with problems, budgets, targets, and staff relations. The same kind of approach to training can be used as with senior managers, but the kinds of problems that can be introduced as a basis for discussion or role play should ideally be those relevant to their own field or level of decision-making.

Technical staff as learners

The term 'technical staff' is intended to cover in broad terms those people who have come from an engineering or other specialized background. It could include medical researchers in the pharmaceuticals industry, chemists in the oil/petrochemicals industry, or computer specialists in the data-processing department of almost any industry. They may be appointed to managerial positions, which means that they will require all the skills mentioned on page 58, while also needing to talk in much more specific detail about highly technical aspects of their work. They may be working in the research and development department of their company and be required to co-operate with other departments, such as marketing, or be able to communicate with clients or joint venture partners outside their own company. They may be team leaders or project managers with responsibility for developing a new product, for example, or seeing a construction project carried out or a new data-processing system installed.

Because of the specialized nature of their work, these learners usually do best in a one-to-one teaching situation. However, their companies may be unwilling to pay extra for individual tuition, and they frequently turn up in non-homogeneous groups where it is difficult to give enough attention to their particular needs.

The problem for these people will be to communicate complex ideas which may be hard for those outside their field to comprehend fully. They therefore need excellent communication strategies, such as: addressing the needs of the listener and choosing appropriate terminology; being aware of how much others can or cannot understand and being ready to explain things in different words; and being able to structure and organize information clearly. Unfortunately, many technical staff have not developed these strategies if they have previously worked in an isolated, monolingual situation. Many have not taken much interest in language before, and may resent the new demands placed on them which they feel inadequate to fulfil.

It is simplistic to regard the needs of these learners purely in terms of vocabulary. Except at very low levels, the technical terminology is rarely a difficulty: most learners already know the technical terms relating to their jobs, and many of these terms may well be universal anyway. The training priority should be to develop confidence in speaking and interacting with others. The trainer can play a useful role in challenging the technical learner to explain ideas in a way that a non-specialist can follow.

Technical staff may be more individualist than managerial staff. They are less likely to have experience of social contacts with regard to their job, so this may be a priority area for them.

Skills that are normally required by technical staff are:

– participating in meetings (usually informal)
– giving presentations
– describing and explaining things or giving instructions to others.

Some will need negotiating skills. They are also likely to need to read technical manuals or specifications, reports, and sometimes contracts. Some may need to write some of these documents.

Typical language areas that will be important for technical staff are: structure, process, function, cause and effect, advantages and disadvantages, and problem-solving (involving hypothesis, possibility/probability, and deduction).

Secretaries and clerical workers as learners

Secretaries

Secretarial positions vary according to the level of the company at which the secretary works. Executive secretaries act as assistants to senior managers and usually carry a lot of responsibility. Some are in frequent contact (both face-to-face and on the telephone) with people from other countries, and are required to have advanced language skills with a high degree of refinement. Departmental secretaries may not have much need for English unless it is an export department or one which deals internationally, but they may occasionally receive telephone calls or have to write letters in English.

Courses for groups of secretaries can be highly efficient because it is possible to draw up a list of skills and language areas that are common to nearly everyone. These include telephoning, writing letters, memos, and faxes, and dealing with visitors to the office. Any differences in needs that do arise within a group will mostly be due to differences in starting level and the degree of language refinement required in different jobs.

Secretaries have the following needs: to be accurate, to use appropriate levels of politeness, and to know conventions and formulaic language. When dealing with visitors, they are likely to be performing definable roles: welcoming, offering hospitality, responding to requests, and perhaps describing the company. If they attend meetings, it will normally be to take minutes rather than to put forward their own ideas. If these points are borne in mind, it can be seen that they will require practice in very different kinds of activities from managerial staff and it is not recommended that groups should be formed to include both managers and secretaries.

Clerical workers

This is a very broad category and the title may not be entirely correct for some of the groups we have included here. They are: receptionists, telephonists, book-keepers and accounts clerks, sales support staff, import–export staff, computer operators, and many others. Their needs for English may be quite specific and will vary according to the type of job. Depending on the country of origin and the education system in that country, workers in these kinds of jobs may have little or no English to start with. They will therefore need basic language training first and foremost. They will probably also need special vocabulary—for example, for understanding computer manuals or following instructions that are written in English; or they may need accountancy or export terms. Those who have to communicate by telephone or fax will need to learn appropriate expressions plus the skills to deal with occasional non-routine situations. Apart from receptionists, not many will have face-to-face dealings with people from other countries.

Few clerical workers are given the chance to attend language training courses. Most companies (fortunately not all) are unwilling to spend money on sending them to language schools in the United Kingdom and if they are given time off to attend a course, this will probably be in a group, in-company. If they are lucky, the group they join will consist of similar people with similar needs. The bigger and more forward-looking companies will try to provide relevant training in homogeneous groups. For example, staff may have the opportunity to join a course in telephone skills or in reading computer manuals. Sometimes a departmental group may have their own English course so that they can focus on the language areas needed for their specific work. If such opportunities do not exist, then these learners will probably end up following a very general type of course and will have to teach themselves the language of the job as they go along.

Departmental differences

This section deals with some typical departments within a company and with the different concerns and training needs of the people who belong to them. The company organogram (Figure 7.1) opposite illustrates how different jobs and departments fit into the overall structure of a large manufacturing company.

Figure 7.1: Company organogram

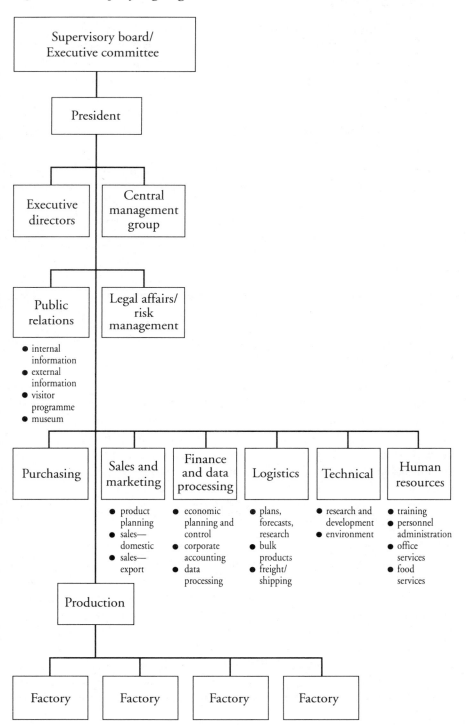

Marketing and sales

First, it is important to recognize the difference between marketing and sales. Marketing staff make decisions or proposals about product development based on analysis of the market and the position which they hope these products will occupy in the market (for example, high quality, low volume, niche category or high volume, low price). They also make decisions about marketing strategies. For example, they will be concerned with ways to promote the image of products and the image of the company as a whole.

In addition to the department manager, the department will probably consist of: product managers, who have special responsibility for one product or one range of products; market researchers; and assistants who carry out the day-to-day administrative work of the department.

Sales staff are concerned with setting and meeting sales targets. The department manager will be looking for ways to motivate sales staff by setting realistic targets and by offering incentives to achieve higher sales. Selling methods are important, and big companies employ their own sales trainers to improve the sales techniques of their staff. To improve customer relations, the more experienced and successful sales staff may be given responsibility for certain important clients, and will then be called 'account managers'.

The sales department may be organized according to sales regions, or type of product, or both. In addition to the sales staff who work in the field, there will also be support staff who answer telephone enquiries and provide information about technical details, purchasing procedures, insurance. Other staff will process orders and pass on information to the accounts department for invoicing, and to dispatch for organizing delivery of products. If the products are being exported, the arrangements concerning transportation, customs declarations, insurance, payment, and delivery schedules will require a lot of documentation.

Not many people are involved in direct selling in a foreign country because in most cases local sales staff are employed or agents are used to make the initial contact. Most sales talk is therefore done in the mother tongue. However, sales and marketing managers working internationally will frequently need to meet and negotiate contractual terms with clients. In multinational companies, sales managers and regional sales managers are regularly required to report to headquarters on the sales situation, and this has to be done in English if the language of the company is English. Sometimes, reporting takes place at a meeting where each representative is required to make a presentation to the others; sometimes the information is given in a written report or is entered into the computer database. The main areas of language here will be: describing trends; comparing budgets with actual figures; giving reasons for fluctuations; reporting on competitors; and making suggestions for increasing sales and market share.

Senior sales or marketing managers will be involved in strategy meetings or in inter-departmental meetings concerning the company as a whole. Sales and marketing staff may require English in order to attend training which has been organized by the parent company at an international level. The training may concern a new product which is due to be launched, or it may concern sales and marketing strategies in general. Sometimes a product launch may involve an international sales congress at a hotel.

Sales and marketing staff are used to dealing with a lot of different people and are usually sociable and have outgoing personalities. On training courses, they respond well to having plenty of activity and opportunities for interaction.

Human resources

Smaller companies will have a personnel department: in a large company, the personnel function is part of a much wider function known as human resources.

A human resources department looks at the potential of its employees for different kinds of work. Human resources staff will try to identify not just the high-flyers, but also the particular talents of junior and middle managers, technical staff, secretaries, and clerical staff. When job vacancies arise, most companies will try to fill them internally first and will look to recruitment only when they need extra numbers or a talent that is lacking among existing staff. Appraising the staff may be done by the use of psychological tests or by annual appraisal interviews. This work is normally carried out in the mother tongue unless there is an international workforce.

Sometimes, in a company which has overseas plant and subsidiaries, there is a need to send staff on assignments abroad for periods of up to five years. The human resources department will then have responsibility for determining the working and living conditions in the foreign country, briefing the employees and, if necessary, their partners, about the country, and taking care of their needs while they are overseas. The staff who do this will need to travel themselves to collect information and build relationships with key people in the other country. Thus there will be a requirement for them to be competent in another language, very often English.

Another important area within the human resources field is training. Large companies will have an extensive training programme for developing their staff in technical skills, management skills, personal development skills, and of course language skills. A training manager will have responsibility for setting up the training programme and overseeing the work of the trainers, who may be employees or external consultants. There may be one training manager or several, depending on the size of the training programme and the number of employees. Many training departments operate as independent profit centres and literally have to sell their courses to other departments. Because training managers have to deal with consultants and training organizations from outside—often from abroad—they frequently have a need for English.

The more commonly known personnel functions involve setting up pay structures and working conditions for different types of jobs within the company. Personnel managers are therefore at the centre of any dispute between employees and management concerning these issues. They are involved in union negotiations and arbitration. Again, these functions do not normally require knowledge of a foreign language.

If personnel or human resources managers require English training, it is usually because they work in a multinational company and have to attend meetings with their counterparts from other countries to decide on policy. They may also need English to attend training courses abroad or international conferences.

Thus these learners will want very broad communication skills at an advanced level, especially for listening to talks, discussing problems, and participating in meetings. Sometimes they will need to make presentations or short speeches. They may want to be able to introduce a consultant at the start of a training session or to chair discussions. They will want to address the issues and problems that most concern them: for example, job motivation, leadership qualities, team building, career development, and job parity.

Finance

The finance department of a big company is normally divided according to different activities and concerns. A clear line can be drawn between accounting and financial planning or control.

Accounting

The majority of finance staff will be employed to deal with day-to-day accounting. At the lowest level, clerical staff deal with payment of invoices, or with the issuing of invoices for sales of the company's products or services. Others calculate all incoming and outgoing transactions and provide information on cashflow. They need to collect and consolidate figures from different departments in the company. Accountants are more highly qualified people who set up and monitor the procedures for dealing with the figures. There may be non-routine situations where decisions have to be made about how and where to record special kinds of income or expenditure. The company will also want to present the figures in the most advantageous light with regard to tax liability, and the senior accountants will be experienced in looking for ways to do this. Accounts departments have to produce financial reports monthly as well as annually, and accounts from the subsidiaries have to be sent to head office to be consolidated into the accounts for the company as a whole.

The need for English normally arises where the company is a multi-national and financial reporting is required to be done in English. Information about accounting procedures may also be distributed to the subsidiaries in English. In this situation, accounts staff will need to know all the relevant accounting terms in English and will need to be able to read instructions about accounting procedures. Some may have to receive visitors from head office or from other subsidiaries and be able to explain aspects of their work. Staff dealing with payments may have to send letters in English to demand payment, or use English to telephone or fax to follow up problems. Senior staff and management will have to write reports in English, and will need to attend meetings with their counterparts from other subsidiaries, or with head office.

Trainers who teach English to accountants and accounts staff will require a basic knowledge of accounting procedures and accounting terms. With job-experienced learners, it is better to find out what procedures the client company uses than to study the British system, because there are many different national (and company) systems. Written documents outlining company accounting procedures, as well as examples of accounts, can usually be obtained to help prepare for a specific course. It will be important to acquire a good Business English dictionary (see Suggestions for Further Reading), or a dictionary of accounting terms.

Financial control

Financial control functions will include: short- and long-term financial planning; investments, movement of capital, acquisitions or sales of assets, calculating return on investment, managing loans, and managing the company pension fund.

Financial planning will normally be carried out by senior managers or directors of the company. However, they will need efficient data support if they are to make good decisions. Thus a large company may employ a team of economic experts to follow trends in markets, prices, equities, interest rates, and exchange rates. These staff will work mainly with on-line data systems in order to get the most up-to-date information; but they may also get information from written financial reports or news-papers such as the *Financial Times*. They will therefore need reading skills combined with a good knowledge of the specific and often colourful ter-minology used to describe trends. If reporting has to be done in English, then writing skills or oral presentation skills will also be important.

Some staff may also carry out transactions: for example, applying to banks for loans, switching loans to take advantage of lower interest rates or more favourable exchange rates, and buying and selling stock. They will also need to have up-to-the-minute information and will probably be in fre-quent contact with banks and other finance institutions worldwide. They will need a high level of confidence and competence in order to exchange information and negotiate deals quickly and efficiently, usually by tele-phone.

Yet other staff may specialize in acquisitions. They may look for smaller companies with useful skills and products that the group could profitably buy, either wholly or on a part-ownership basis. They may specialize in property, plant, or other kinds of investment. These staff will need to travel and to carry out detailed research into the financial pros and cons of each prospective investment. Where the investment is planned in an over-seas location, the need for English to make contacts and collect informa-tion will again be paramount.

The people to be found in these financial control functions will be highly qualified and expert in their own field. They therefore belong more to the technical staff category (see page 60) than the managerial staff category (see page 57), although of course some eventually become department heads and senior managers.

Production

This department is relevant in companies where there is a physical prod-uct, and a manufacturing process is involved in producing it.

There will be a large number of people who are engaged in the physical manufacture of the product. Only where there is a multinational work-force will there be any need for such workers to learn English. A typical example where English is required is within the oil industry. There is often a large number of expatriate workers in oil- or gas-processing plants in the Middle East or the Far East, and locally-employed operatives need to communicate with them to report on and solve production problems. They may also need to follow training in English. Their needs will be nar-row, highly focused, and technical rather than business-orientated.

In most cases, however, it is only the managerial staff who are likely to require English language skills. If a company has overseas plants, managers may be sent from the parent company to oversee the production and make sure that the activities are carried out in line with company policy. Even if the language of the country is not English, English may still be used as the medium of communication. These managers will be involved in building good staff relations with the local employees, and co-operating with them to solve production problems. They may have specific responsibilities such as modernizing the plant or improving quality or productivity. They will need to be very familiar with all the language relating to the process itself, but probably more important will be the language and skills required to relate to the foreign culture and develop a good understanding of the people. Senior managers working overseas may have a lot of social obligations: they will probably be expected to attend formal functions with local dignitaries and government officials as well as other expatriates such as embassy staff. Thus they will have a need for formal social language such as the language of entertaining.

Production managers working in their own country may also need English from time to time, particularly in relation to purchasing. In larger companies, there is usually a purchasing department, which may belong to the production department, or may be independent. All manufacturing companies need to purchase both raw materials and production equipment, from expensive machinery to nuts and bolts. A number of staff may be employed to research prices and negotiate deals for the lower-cost items and one-off purchases. Either the production manager or the purchasing manager may be involved in negotiating for the more expensive items, or for larger contracts with long-term suppliers. Here, obviously, negotiation skills will be of prime importance and an advanced level of English will be needed to negotiate with foreign suppliers. As many negotiations are carried out over the telephone, telephoning skills will often be important as well. Purchasing staff will also need to be able to read the technical specifications of a product, and at higher levels they will need to understand and negotiate supply contracts.

Other functions that the production manager will be responsible for include the setting and meeting of production targets, reviewing budgets and production methods, controlling quality, and improving productivity. In a multinational company, the production manager may need to attend planning meetings in which these areas are discussed. He or she will probably need to report regularly to head office, giving the latest production figures and forecasting the figures for the coming months. Thus meetings skills and reporting skills will be important, and learners will need to be able to describe trends, forecast, compare targets with actual figures, and describe the causes and effects of problems.

Another important area relating to production is the field of transport and storage of goods. In the first place, raw materials needed for the process have to be brought to the manufacturing site and stored prior to use. At the other end of the process, the finished goods have to be stored and then transported to the customer, perhaps via an intermediary such as a distributor or retailer. In recent years, transport and storage has become a high-technology activity. With modern computer technology, it is possible to achieve 'just-in-time' delivery whereby the storage space and storage time can be limited to the absolute minimum, thus saving costs. A large company may have a logistics department or materials-handling department which deals exclusively with this activity. Purchasers will need to be familiar with company procedures in order to negotiate favourable delivery terms. Managers will be looking for ways to update the system and streamline the process even further. All employees dealing with this area will need skills for describing process and procedure, and for making comparisons between old and new systems.

This analysis of jobs within a typical company cannot, of course, cover every possibility. We have not attempted to cover specific industries or service sectors, many of which have their own organizational features and a highly specific terminology (for example, banking and insurance). However, it is intended that this should provide a framework into which a Business English trainer can fit the knowledge and experience he or she acquires on the job.

8 INFORMATION GATHERING

We have seen that the chief tenet of Business English is to relate training to needs, but in order to do that it is first necessary to establish what those needs are.

We have so far looked at two key areas of needs. In Chapter 6, we looked at how to define the training gap by assessing the level of ability the learner has so far acquired and the target level which is needed for a specific purpose. Chapter 7 addressed the kinds of specific purposes which Business English learners are likely to have. By looking at different categories of jobs, we saw how it is possible to predict some of the skills and training requirements of learners.

To develop an efficient course, however, we need to select key components, appropriate materials, and relevant tasks and activities which will develop the learners and achieve the objectives. This requires a much more detailed knowledge of the learners' needs.

Success in learning can only come about if the learner is motivated. Making the course relevant to job or study needs is usually a good way to motivate the learner. However, there may be a few learners who are not interested in talking about their specialization, or may not want to study the language relating to it. If such a case arises, then a key part of the needs analysis will be to find out what will motivate the learner. The diplomatic trainer can still find ways to practise valuable language skills and language areas (excepting specialist vocabulary) through materials and activities that stimulate the learner's interest.

What do we need to know?

Information about the learner

This is information about factors which could affect the learner's response to training, motivation, and learning potential. These factors are:

- General personal data: age, sex, nationality, mother tongue
- Educational background: academic, professional, and vocational
- Knowledge of other languages and other language learning experience
- Attitudes and assumptions about language learning
- Learning style: for example, does the learner prefer to think problems through and try to fit new information into a coherent system (a theorist), or does he or she like to try ideas out and see how they work in practice (a pragmatist); is he or she someone who needs time to think before reaching conclusions (a reflector), or does he or she need to be actively involved in doing something 'at all times (an activist)? (See Honey and Mumford (1986) for more details.)

Defining the learning purpose

In the case of job-experienced learners, this will be a breakdown of what the learners do in their jobs. For pre-experience learners, there will be at least two sets of needs: those relating to the study situation (following courses, passing examinations) and those relating to their future careers.

In both categories, the key features that are important in defining the learning purpose will be as follows:

- Activities and tasks: what the learner has to do in English
- Interaction: who the learner communicates with; the roles they each play; the relationship between them
- Topic: what they communicate about
- Attitudes and tones likely to be expressed (for example, formal, polite, strong, tentative)
- Mode of interaction (for example, letter, telephone call, face-to-face)
- Setting: place, time of day, time limits, and other situational factors which influence the interaction.

Information about the learning situation

The trainer is frequently assigned to a course that has been set up without his or her involvement. However, understanding the forces at work behind a training programme can be vital for its success, particularly if there is any conflict between the various protagonists.

Questions to be asked are:

- Who decided that the learner should attend this course?
- What training needs does the learner perceive?
- What training needs does the sponsor perceive?
- What are the constraints of the learning situation: time, budget, group size, group membership, assessment and evaluation procedures, stated objectives?

Ways of gathering the information

The next two sections will look at ways of gathering the information listed here.

Job-experienced learners

Information can be gathered at three different stages in the training process: (1) before the course begins; (2) at the start of the course; and (3) during the course.

Before the course begins

Methods of gathering information before the start of a course will depend on the physical situation. If the distance between the training organization and the learner is great, then the information will have to pass by telephone or by the written word. Questionnaires are the most convenient method for collecting information. A standard questionnaire can be prepared by the training organization for use with typical clients and participants. This can be sent by mail or fax, and the participant can fill it in in his or her own time and return it. Questionnaires are useful for providing the participant's personal details, educational background, and previous language learning experience; they can also elicit brief information about the job and the job skills which the learner sees as important. For example, a checklist of job skills could be included and the learner asked to tick those which he or she needs to work on. The learner might also be asked to assess his or her level on a simple scale. In addition, some open-ended questions can be constructed which will provide some indication of the learner's ability in English (for example, 'Write a brief description of your job').

In addition to a questionnaire, it may be possible for the trainer or training organization to talk to the sponsor (for example, company training manager) or even to the course participants themselves. Although this is time-consuming and expensive, it is useful for establishing the sponsor's and the learner's level. If the physical distance is small enough, the trainer might be able to visit the company before a course starts, and talk directly to the learners and/or others involved in setting up the course. Sometimes the learner's immediate superior can be useful in pinpointing his or her needs and problems. Training managers may or may not have a very detailed picture of learners' needs, depending on their own professional background, knowledge of language training, and knowledge of English.

After analysing questionnaires and (if applicable) talking to the sponsor, the trainer may wish to carry out some further background research. This could include learning more about the company by reading company literature or articles about the company in the press. It could include research into the type of industry the learners are involved in (for example, banking, insurance, pharmaceuticals). Sometimes, learners can be asked to supply information about their work by sending in examples of documents which they commonly use: product specifications, contracts, memos, or technical reports, for instance. These can be analysed both for content and for the type of language they represent.

If a trainer is not familiar with the country or region that the learner comes from, it may be helpful to learn more about the place and also about the cultural background. It will be useful to know what kind of behaviour patterns, learning attitudes, or language learning difficulties could be expected.

The information which a trainer has access to before a course will vary considerably. Sometimes key information will be missing, and the trainer will have to rely on assumptions and intelligent guesswork in order to put together an outline programme before the course begins.

At the start of the course

Clearly it becomes much easier to establish the needs and objectives of the learners once they are on-site and can talk face to face. However, the extent to which needs and course objectives can be discussed with the learners will depend on the training situation and on the type of course being run.

Open group courses

A typical feature of open group courses is that they contain a mixture of participants. Learners may have been assigned to the group on the basis of their level of language, but it is quite likely that they will have very differing needs in terms of job-specific skills, topic interests, and language areas. Thus the course will have rather broad objectives and it will not be worthwhile carrying out a detailed needs analysis when specific needs cannot be met.

However, it is still important to get to know each learner well and to give each a chance to talk about his or her own particular interests. Since it would be time-consuming and boring for other learners if the trainer were to interview each member individually, one approach in a group course is to have learners interview each other about, for example, their companies, their jobs, and their products (if applicable). The interviews can be controlled by preparing interview task sheets that focus on the areas to be covered. One or two examples of these are given at the end of this chapter.

While the learners are interviewing each other, the trainer can circulate among the pairs and note down any useful information that comes out of the activity. The learners can also be asked to summarize the information for the whole group. It is a useful language activity and also helps the learners to learn more about each other.

Closed groups

Depending on the rationale for bringing the group together, it is much more likely that a closed group will have specific objectives that have already been defined before the course starts. Most of the groundwork in analysing needs and setting up a course programme will already have been carried out. However, if the learners do not know each other, it could still be useful to carry out the interview activity as described above. Alternatively, the course could begin with a discussion session in which learners can talk about their own needs and reasons for attending the course. This can work very well if the members of the group already know each other and feel reasonably relaxed. There is a danger, however, that different opinions will be expressed about what the course should cover, and the trainer will be left with the dilemma of trying to reconcile opposing points of view.

Individual tuition

In individual tuition, more than in any other teaching situation, needs analysis is an integral part of the course and vital to its success. Depending on the length of the course and the complexity of the learner's needs, it could be worthwhile to spend two or three hours on needs analysis at the start of the course.

Most of this needs analysis will take the form of a trainer-learner interview. Although the trainer may have some information about the learner from, say, a completed questionnaire, it will still be important to check, verify, and collect more details about the job and language needs.

Questions that can be asked at such an interview may focus on such details as:

- The company: its size, location of its offices, what different divisions there are, where its subsidiaries are, its products or services, and markets
- The division or department where the learner works
- The job which the learner does
- What the learner does in English: what skills needs he or she has, what he or she talks about and to whom
- What he or she feels are priorities with regard to English training; what are the main difficulties, and so on.

Included here are some extracts from actual needs analysis interviews as examples of the kinds of questions that can be asked, and the likely responses.

Extract 1

L I have been working for [Company] since 2 years now, for 2 years now, and I use a lot of English in my work, and I need to be more comfortable in my English speaking because I have some net-working, some meetings in English, some presentations to do, and that's why I'm here.

T Okay, so you say you use English a lot in your work, do you use English . . .?

L I use English everyday, I think, but, sometimes ten minutes each day, but sometimes it is all the week. In meetings in London or Bruxelles I need to speak English.

T And on this daily basis, who do you speak to?

L I speak to American people, English people, also with Dutch people.

T And does this commonly take place by telephone or face-to-face?

L Most of . . . it takes place by telephone, and day to day by tele-phone, and of course if it's a meeting or presentation it's face-to-face.

T And how often do you have these meetings—where you have to speak in English?

L I think it's almost once a month we have a meeting or presenta-tion to do, or once a couple of months.

T Okay. And how many people will attend?

L Generally this meeting, it depends, but no more than ten people, no more ten persons in this meetings.

T And what sort of things are talked about?

L I talk about problems concerning our chemical unit. I talk about figures. I talk about . . .

T What, production figures?

L Yes, production figures. What we are expecting. What we expect for the next month. What we are and where we go.

Extract 2

T You seem to have quite a good level already. Obviously the time you spent in the States was useful.

L Yes, well actually, as a lot of French people I attended English courses during my normal scholarity, but I couldn't say that at this stage my English was very good. Then I started my profes-sional career. I didn't speak a lot of English during the first one or two years. This was back in 1975.

I've always been based in Paris, but I travelled a lot to the US, particularly in New York, but also in Houston, but it's probably on that occasion that I practised my English more frequently. But I also had, have as you may imagine, a lot of meetings with English or American bankers, so in Paris I speak frequently English either in meetings or by telephone, not necessarily with English-speaking people, I mean native English-speaking people, but also with Dutch or German or Japanese, which may create . . .

T Well, that's one of the interesting things about English.
L That's right, that's right. Absolutely.
T It's an international language.
L As for my professional language, this is probably an area where I'm not too worried because these are really the same words in French and English. I may make presentations, or listen to a presentation of a particular financing technique without any real difficulty. My real difficulty is to understand and participate to a marginal conversation.
T I think what you are saying is that when you are sure of the context, there is no problem.
L Yes, that's right . . . but also language, because if you speak very rapidly I'm afraid I will not understand you . . . but you are right. It is difficult to separate what corresponds to learning of a foreign language and integration in different contexts and environments.
T Your English is very good.
L Well, maybe because it's the morning. In the evening, I could have some difficulty, sometimes.

Both these speakers have a good knowledge of English, though there is no doubt that the second speaker is much more fluent. He is accurate and precise in his reference to time. He uses an abundance of markers, such as 'well', 'actually', and 'I mean'. He responds promptly and with confidence: 'That's right, that's right. Absolutely.' His reaction to the compliment at the end is without hesitation. He has, however, certain recognizable elements of mother tongue interference.

The two interviews illustrate two different sets of needs. The first speaker wants to feel more comfortable in a business environment—in meetings and presentations. The second speaker says very definitely that he has other needs—the problems that arise in marginal situations, where the context is not clear to him. For the first trainer, the approach is clear. The focus should be on the language of meetings and presentations. The second trainer must avoid the irrelevance of the slight mother tongue interference: one or two weeks of expensive training is only going to make a marginal difference to this. The main focus is going to be on helping the learner to deal with unfamiliar contexts, and the development of conversational and social strategies.

Extract 3

In the third extract, a middle manager in a German car manufacturing company describes his career.

> L I start in 1965 in the factory and I'm working for one machine for two years. After two years I change my job and I start to the small leader in one department and repair machines and, and, and do anythings what is found in the machines and so on. In 1970, I go straight to supervisor and I start in supervisor in department wh— pressing . . . and I worked there for six years to 1978. In 1978 I go over again to other department also for one supervision, only the different machines there for for . . . I don't know . . . I don't know the name. In 1980 I go from [name of factory] to Nigeria and I'm working there in the final assembly for the section manager and in 1948 [*sic*] I come back from Nigeria and I start in [factory name], also for supervisor in one department who's welding axle. And after this I'm working there only for six or seven months. My big boss is coming and say OK you must go to one new department is going up in [name of town] and I do this job for 1985 to 1990.

Commentary

This extract illustrates clearly a learner who has learned English on the job without the benefit of a grounding in English at school. He is now 50 years old and is unlikely to make dramatic improvement in terms of accuracy. He is outgoing and communicative, and speaks fluently, but his output is often full of inaccuracies. His trainer will need to take a firm hand to slow him down and make him aware of the language areas in which he makes mistakes. He will need a pragmatic approach: not all his errors can be targeted, so the focus should be on the ones that hinder effective communication most. (For example, giving the date wrongly, "working for one machine"—these are errors that could cause most confusion for the listener.) He will need constant correction and reminders, and even then will probably continue to make many habitual errors.

During the course

At the start of the course, or soon after, the trainer must evaluate all the information that has been collected and must make certain deductions which will determine the objectives for the course. These objectives should ideally be agreed by the learners.

Thus the outlines for the course will be laid down, but it will still be very difficult to plan all the details of the content and materials to be covered in the course. This is because the trainer is constantly learning more about the learners as the course progresses. First, information about job-specific topics and language may be complex and detailed, and not everything can be covered in a couple of hours. Second, some information will be sensitive, and the learners will not want to divulge this unless an environment of trust and confidence has built up over a period of time. Third, some information relating to the learners, such as attitudes to language learning, motivation, and learning styles, cannot easily be discussed and is generally communicated through behaviour during the course.

Thus the trainer must be constantly responsive to new information that emerges during a course and must be ready to adapt course content and approach to deal with it. Even the most tightly-prepared course can be modified—for example, by pruning the least useful parts, adding new material or activities, increasing or decreasing the emphasis placed on a particular aspect, or changing the order of components.

The trainer can also make specific efforts to add to his or her knowledge of the learner's situation by introducing discussions or carrying out short interviews during the course.

Information that can be gained during the course includes:

1 More details of specific work situations

For example: when the learner attends monthly meetings at head office, who else is present? What do they talk about? What happened at the last meeting? What kinds of problems were discussed? What solutions did they reach? This kind of information will provide a useful basis for setting discussion topics and building up role plays based on real-life situations.

2 More details about the work done by the learner

For example: how does a risk surveyor set about assessing the risks in a client company? Who does he or she talk to and what questions does he or she ask? What vocabulary is needed to fill out forms?

This kind of information will provide useful clues as to the functional, structural, and lexical areas of language needed to carry out various job tasks.

Pre-experience learners

The needs of pre-experience learners are quite distinct from those of job-experienced learners, and the approach to needs analysis will therefore be very different.

Generally speaking, it will not be left to the individual trainer to set up the training objectives, course curriculum, or course design. These decisions will either be determined by an examining body (internal or external), or they will be made by senior members of the department, and will be formalized and carried on from one year to another with perhaps only minor modifications.

Needs will be assessed in general language terms rather than in relation to specific job tasks. In some educational establishments, the language programme may have as its objectives the same kinds of skills as are important in working life: for example, giving presentations, writing letters, telephoning, and participating in discussions. However, there may also be other objectives that relate more specifically to the present need to follow a course of study: for example, reading to extract the main points from an academic text, or following and taking notes on a lecture. The trainer will have to be able to relate the materials and activities used on the course to these objectives, and will be given guidelines for preparing lessons and for evaluating and assessing progress.

In some establishments, the course objectives and its programme will be defined by the course materials used—either a published textbook or internally-prepared material. However, in every case there will be some room for choice of interpretation and selection of activities. The trainer will make such choices according to the needs of particular groups.

Motivation

In any learning situation, we can distinguish between two kinds of motivation: extrinsic (the need is imposed from outside) and intrinsic (the learner is deeply interested in the language and culture for its own sake). Among pre-experience learners, the extrinsic motivation will stem from the need to pass examinations and gain qualifications. Many learners will not be aware of the needs they will have later in life and may not be able to see the relevance of doing language courses. Even if they know they will need English in their future jobs, the need is a distant one, and course participants may not want to devote a lot of time and energy to language when there are so many other stimulating things to get involved in.

Thus, perhaps the main task for the trainer will be to find out what special interests the members of a group have, and what kinds of activities they will best respond to. In this way, the trainer can stimulate interest and increase motivation.

There are several ways of doing this:

1 Introduce open sessions in which group members can talk about what interests them most. Topics that arise can be followed up in later

sessions, with appropriate materials and activities. Even if the topics that come up may not seem very business-related, they can still be used to develop valuable skills.

2 Bring in speakers from outside who are working in relevant fields and who can give the learners an insight into the practical applications of what they are studying. If any members of the group have some work experience, they could be encouraged to tell the others about it.

3 Encourage the group to talk about their attitudes to language learning and about any difficulties they have. Discuss the problems openly and suggest strategies that may help.

4 Be ready to try out different kinds of tasks and activities, especially those that actively involve the learners and develop useful skills. Those that were successful can be repeated, using different topics.

Practical problems in needs analysis

Needs analysis is rarely straightforward. Below are some typical examples of problems, and some suggestions for dealing with them.

1 Companies do not supply the information you need

Solutions

Try to build a relationship with someone inside the company: usually it will be the training manager or personnel manager, but it could be a secretary or assistant. Explain the importance of getting information about the needs of course participants and get him or her to help you to obtain that information by liaising with appropriate departments or personnel.

2 Companies see the training requirements differently from the learner or the training organization

Solutions

1 Try to negotiate with the person or people who are most influential in setting up the training.

2 If this doesn't work, try to reconcile the differences: steer a middle course that satisfies both parties to some degree.

3 Aim to satisfy the needs of the learners first: training is unlikely to continue in the face of poor evaluation.

3 The course objectives that have been laid down are inappropriate for the group

Solutions

1 Discuss with the group what they see as their main objectives. Match this with your own professional judgement of what they need. Change the course programme accordingly.

2 If this is impossible—(for example, it is an examination course or the sponsor refuses to change the programme)—you will have to stick to the given course outline, but you could try to spend some class time on areas that relate more closely to the needs of the learners.

4 The needs within a group are too divergent

This is a very common problem. There may be differences in level or in job requirements, or it may be a question of strongly opposed personalities or different learning styles.

Solutions

1 In the majority of cases, the trainer has to try to manage somehow by finding the middle road.

2 If the problem is one of level, aim at the learners in the middle for most of the time. It may be possible to devote some extra time to helping the lower-level learners while the others are preparing something more difficult. Some tasks and activities allow for participation at different levels. For example, chairing a meeting is more challenging than being a participant, and it makes sense, therefore, to give the role of the chair to a higher-level member of the group.

3 If the problem is one of different job requirements, focus on the common core of needs—don't try to address all the specific needs of individuals. Some activities will allow individuals to talk about their own interests—for example, interviews and presentations, and of course writing tasks.

4 In the case of different personalities, discuss the problem openly with the group and try to agree on some common ground. It is useful to point out that different people have different learning styles and that sometimes, in a group, there is a need for the faster or more active learners to be patient while the others catch up. This kind of discussion will not solve the problem, but it may help to make the group members more tolerant of each other.

5 In extreme cases, it may be possible to change the group or divide it into two.

6 Another solution could be to introduce self-study sessions and pull people out for short periods of individual tuition.

7 Another possibility is to have learners work on different tasks in smaller sub-groups.

5 Some learners do not think they need to attend the course

Solutions

1 Try to demonstrate that they do have needs by setting tasks that they cannot perform adequately: show them the gaps in their knowledge and skills. Recording them on tape is one way to do this. However, an apparent excess of confidence can sometimes be a cover-up for deep feelings of inadequacy. In these cases, it will be necessary to employ a more tactful and gentle approach.

2 Try to find materials and activities that will interest and motivate the learners. Even if there is no genuine need for training, learning can still be enjoyable.

Tables 8.1 to 8.4 on the following pages give examples of interview task sheets which learners can use to ask each other questions about each others' jobs, companies, etc. (See also page 74.)

Examples of interview task sheets

Table 8.1: Interview task sheet—company

Finding out about a company

1 Ask your partner questions about the company where he or she works. Use the headings below as a guide.

2 Make notes about your partner's company and be ready to present the information to the group.

Company name:

Type of business:

Some important products or services:

Location of headquarters:

Approximate number of employees:

Main competitors:

Countries which the company deals with or exports to:

Approximate turnover: (if available)

Table 8.2: Interview task sheet—job

Finding out about a job

1 Ask your partner questions about the company where he or she works. Use the headings below as a guide.

2 Make notes about your partner's company and be ready to present the information to the group.

Job title:

Department:

Brief description of job:

Special responsibilities/special difficulties:

Table 8.3: Interview task sheet—contacts

Finding out about contacts: regular contacts

1 Make a list of people you communicate with regularly in English:

2 Now select one of them and complete the details below:

Name: Company:

Job title: Division/department:

Nationality:

Most frequent means of communication: (circle)

   face-to-face   in meeting with others   telephone   letter/fax

Relationship: (circle)

   friendly   neutral   formal

What do you find most difficult when you try to communicate with this person:

What would help you to communicate better:

Finding out about contacts: new contacts

How often do you make a new contact? (circle)

    every week   *every month*   *occasionally*   *never*

What nationality are the people you make contact with?

How do you usually contact them? (tick)

    You telephone or write for an appointment
    They visit you in your office
    You meet them at international meetings or conferences
    You meet them on social occasions
    Other ways

Describe one person who was a new contact recently:

    Purpose of contact:
    Personal details:
    Company:
    Job title:
    Nationality:
    How did you talk: (circle)   face-to-face   telephone
    What did you find most difficult when you made the contact:

What would help you to make first contact more easily next time:

Table 8.4: Interview task sheet—company product

Finding out about the company's products

Complete the following chart about one of your company's products. Then ask your partner for information about his or her company's products and complete the column on the right.

	You	Your partner
Name of product:		
Market sector:		
Function or use:		
Brief description:		
When introduced:		
Total exports for last year (if available):		
Market share in your country (if available):		
What type of customers buy this product:		
Who are your main competitors:		

Photocopiable material   © Oxford University Press 1994

9 DETERMINING THE CONTENT OF THE COURSE

This chapter will demonstrate how to move from the outline stage (where the course objectives and main performance areas have been identified) to the detailed planning stage (where decisions can be made about what to include and how to deal with it).

There are two approaches to planning. The first is to take each of the main performance areas and break it down into its constituent parts: skills components, language functions, and the grammatical and lexical constituents. The second approach is to analyse the language used in samples taken from real life situations, or from simulations of real life situations, such as management training videos or output from the learners themselves (even though that may be imperfect). Here, also, the analysis yields the key functions, structures, and features of language which a learner needs to know: but the process involves observation rather than deduction.

Breakdown of performance areas

In this section, a breakdown is given of five broad performance areas:

1 Meetings and discussions

2 Giving information

3 Telephoning

4 Business correspondence

5 Socializing.

For each area, a checklist of the key functions involved will be given. In addition, there will be: notes on the key parameters which provide the basis for selecting appropriate language from a broad corpus; and notes on other aspects that will be important for successful communication, such as the correct use of underlying structures, stress, and intonation. Vocabulary will not be dealt with in this section as this will depend on the specialization of the learners and the topics they want to talk about. However, some examples of vocabulary are given where their use is highly predictable within a certain functional area.

This breakdown will provide a starting point for selecting the components of almost any Business English course. However, it will be important to carry out the steps of language analysis and to examine carefully the focus of training as outlined on pages 102–111.

Meetings and discussions

This is a very broad performance area covering large, formal meetings, small, informal meetings, and discussions of all kinds. Within this area, three distinct kinds of behaviour can be identified: controlling, participating, and co-operating. Each requires specific kinds of language and language skills.

Controlling

In formal meetings this is the prerogative of the chairperson, but in informal meetings anyone present can contribute to this role. To control the meeting means: (1) making sure that the objectives are achieved (to follow the agenda if there is one); (2) balancing the points of view of the participants and seeing that everyone makes a fair contribution; (3) recognizing and dealing with disruptive influences, such as participants who try to dominate or misunderstandings of word and meaning; (4) operating within agreed time limits; (5) working to a protocol (a management style which is appropriate to the occasion). An example of protocol is where participants are required to speak through the chair.

A good chairperson can only carry out this role if he or she has competence in the language. Not least of the skills requirements is listening, as it is impossible to summarize accurately without having both heard and understood everything. Most meetings do not proceed in a linear fashion because ideas are frequently reiterated, reformulated, and elaborated as the group moves from defining problems towards finding solutions. Participants are often so involved with their own thoughts that they do not perceive the development of ideas within the group as a whole. It is the chairperson's role to point out the development and to summarize key aspects of it.

Language functions relating to controlling meetings are:

- opening the meeting
- nominating topics for discussion
- rejecting topics
- asking people to speak
- keeping people on the subject
- postponing a topic
- coming back to a topic
- referring to time
- summarizing, restating, or rephrasing
- concluding
- closing the meeting.

In identifying the appropriate choice of expression for carrying out these functions, a key parameter will be formality versus informality (for example, 'I declare this meeting open'; 'Right, let's get started').

The structures which learners will need to be familiar with are (broadly): modal verbs, verb tenses, conditional forms, connectors (for example, because, therefore, alternatively).

Participating

As with controlling meetings, the most essential skill involved in successful participation in meetings is listening. This is often overlooked in training, or at any rate is given less emphasis than the skills of putting forward arguments and showing disagreement. Thus, each of the functions listed below should be seen as two-way: learners will need to express these transactions (though not necessarily overtly), but they will also need to understand and respond to the transactions of others.

There are some kinds of behaviours that are inappropriate in some cultures: for example, disagreeing or criticizing is not acceptable in some Far East countries. It is important to be aware of differences in behaviour when dealing with people from an unfamiliar culture.

Language functions relating to participating in meetings:

- negotiating procedure
- setting out facts and figures
- expressing opinions
- supporting an argument
- agreeing, disagreeing
- expressing reservation
- adding new points
- balancing points of view
- expressing advantages/disadvantages
- making suggestions

- evading, postponing, ignoring
- interrupting
- promising.

A key parameter in the choice of language will be diplomacy versus force-fulness: for example, in making a proposal or expressing degrees of agree-ment or disagreement ('Could I suggest . . .'; 'You must . . .'; 'I'm not sure if I can go along with that'; 'That's unacceptable').

The structures will be the same as for controlling meetings.

Co-operating

Co-operating is a major factor in international meetings where English is being used by non-native speakers. The principles of co-operation will be to reduce extreme forms of language and behaviour, and to establish a neutral middle ground where people from different backgrounds can communicate. The term co-operating is taken from the concept of 'co-operative principles', first used by Grice (1975). It is used in the restricted sense of co-operation through language and behaviour in order to achieve a mutually desirable business objective.

The language of clarifying is an important aspect of co-operating. In an atmosphere of co-operation, the assumption is that members of a meeting will first try to understand and relate to the others, and second, will try to work with the others to find solutions to common problems.

One aspect of co-operating behaviour is when the speaker notices that others have not understood and stops to rephrase or restate a point, or even to check ('Did you understand?'). Listeners can show understanding by giving various forms of feedback such as nodding the head, or inter-jecting with 'Hmm' or 'Right', or by repeating parts of what they heard. British and American participants use such devices all the time and expect others to do the same. However, in some cultures it is not appropriate to make noises while others are speaking; or it may be seen as a criticism of the speaker to say that you have not understood. These people may have to learn to change their behaviour in the context of an international meet-ing in order that the meeting can progress satisfactorily.

In the list of functions below, reference is made to following rituals and routines, and these terms need to be defined.

Rituals are important for business people working internationally because they meet a wide variety of different people, in situations where time is often a constraint. Rituals provide clear ground rules for meetings, enabling people to feel comfortable with one another in a short space of time. Rituals include: welcoming, introducing, small talk before a meet-ing, formal thanks, and saying goodbye. The language used in these rituals is often highly formalized. Rituals are often affected by cultural parameters. In Latin American countries, for example, more time may be devoted to developing a friendly relationship than in Scandinavia, for example. Even within Europe there can be noticeable differences. In Sweden it is common for a guest to publicly thank, or propose a toast to, his host or hostess at a dinner table. In Britain, this public thanking is not seen as necessary, although it may occur. It can be said that following such ritualistic behaviour greatly enhances business exchanges, while the non-observance of rituals (such as the unwelcome introduction of business topics during a social dinner with Japanese people) can sometimes be destructive to a business relationship.

Routines   are commonly accepted procedures for doing things which are highly predictable. An example is the classic five-point routine for starting a meeting:

1 calling attention

2 signalling the start

3 giving background information

4 stating purpose

5 inviting the first speaker.

Other routines may be used for taking turns to speak, closing meetings, dealing with questions, or interrupting. An important feature of routines is time limit. A routine should only take a certain amount of time, and the participants in a meeting will have certain expectations of the time a routine should take. However, there may be cultural differences in expectations of the time needed for certain routines. For example, greetings in the Middle East go on longer than in Britain. (Note that routines are also important in socializing: see page 101.)

Language functions relating to co-operating in meetings:

– following rituals
– following routines
– clarifying
– checking
– rephrasing or restating to make a point clear
– asking for explanations
– concluding
– showing understanding
– confirming
– referring to time boundaries
– dealing with lack of co-operation.

Key parameters in the choice of language relating to these functions are: formal versus informal; polite versus impolite; neutral forms versus deviant forms. Easy rather than complex language should be chosen if the language level of some participants is low. It will be important to avoid specialist jargon unless it is familiar to everyone present; similarly, company-specific terms, idioms, or language that is highly culture-bound will create divisions rather than co-operation between the different parties.

Key structures will be question forms, especially tag questions, check questions, and statement questions. ('You need more time, is that right?' 'I see, so what you mean is . . .')

Table 9.1: Functions for expressing ideas—structural and vocabulary components

Function	Structures	Vocabulary
describing structure		'consists of', 'divided into', 'whole', 'parts'
describing function		'is used to . . .', 'is used for -ing'
describing process	present tenses, active/passive, sequence markers	
expressing time	verb tenses, adverbials, time prepositions	
expressing condition	conditionals	
describing location, movement, and direction	prepositions, adverbials	
describing change/trends	verb tenses	'increase', 'decrease'
giving reasons, expressing cause and effect		connectors: 'because', 'as a result of', 'therefore'
expressing similarity and difference		'the same as', 'similar to', 'like/unlike'
comparing and contrasting	*-er* and *-est* forms	'more', 'most', 'least'
expressing possibility, probability, and certainty	modal verbs sentence construction	'could', 'may', 'might' 'it is likely that . . .', 'we are likely to . . .'
expressing intention	'will'/'going to'	

Giving information

This performance area relates to several different kinds of communication:

- short items of factual information, given during meetings with one or with several other people
- information given over the telephone
- longer, more structured communications in the form of presentations, talks, or speeches
- written communications such as faxes, letters, memos, and reports.

There are two aspects of giving information: the content, i.e. the ideas to be communicated; and the way in which the message is communicated.

The content of the message

Table 9.1 (opposite) lists the functions that are widely used to communicate different kinds of information in the field of Business English. They may relate to a variety of different topic areas. For example, 'describing structure' is relevant to talking about the structure of a company (its departments/divisions) or the structure of a product. 'Expressing similarity and difference' may be important in talking about product development, differences between the company's products and competitors', or differences between one job function and another.

How the message is communicated

The key feature of communicating a message are: (1) organizing the message, (2) signalling intention, and (3) emphasizing important points.

Organizing the message

This involves both linguistic and non-linguistic skills. The non-linguistic skills relate to how information is selected according to the needs of the audience or readership, and to how the information is ordered—what kind of logical sequence is applied. See Table 9.2 (overleaf).

Signalling intention

This is an important device which a speaker or writer can use to communicate more effectively. By signalling intentions, the speaker can prepare the audience for what is to come. It is a common device in presentations where the speaker introduces a topic ('I'm going to talk to you about . . .') or explains the structure of the talk ('First I will give you some background about . . . and then I will . . .'); and also in meetings ('I'd like to make a suggestion'; 'I have a question about pricing').

Signalling intention is also a useful strategy for breaking down the details of a complex message into manageable components—grammatically simpler to express as well as easier to understand. This is especially useful for

Table 9.2: Functions and linguistic skills for organizing the message

Function	Language
Showing sequence	Sequence markers: 'first', 'second', etc.
Marking boundaries	*Oral:* 'right', 'OK', use of pauses, stress, intonation *Written:* headings, subheadings, paragraphs, sentence boundaries
Marking new/given information	*Oral:* stress and intonation *Written:* use of articles, demonstratives, pronouns *Both:* choice of vocabulary, giving definitions
Referring to what went before or comes later	Use of appropriate expressions: 'as I said', 'the above-mentioned . . .'
Linking and showing the relationship between ideas	Connecting words and phrases: 'however', 'as a result', 'for example'
Referring to visuals or to things outside the text.	*Oral:* 'as you can see . . .' *Written:* 'as is shown in Fig. 8 . . .'.

questions. For example, instead of the complex question, 'Do you sell to any other kinds of companies apart from the big car manufacturers?' we can ask:

'About your customers' (signalling topic)

'I know you sell to the big car manufacturers' (signalling what we already know)

'Who are your other customers?' (actual question).

In written communications, there are different conventions for signalling intention according to the type of communication. In a fax or letter, the subject is indicated by a heading. In memos, there is a standard layout where the writer can indicate in the appropriate box who the memo is for, who it is from, and what it is about. Reports, especially longer ones, usually have an introduction in which the writer specifies his or her intentions and describes the content and structure of the report. In the main body of the report, intentions are signalled by headings (for example, 'Recommendations'), as well as explicit statements ('The following list indicates . . .'; 'Here are some examples'). Table 9.3 lists functions and language used in signalling intentions.

Table 9.3: Functions and linguistic skills for signalling intention

Function	Language
Getting attention	'Ladies and gentlemen'
	'John, can I have a word?'
Stating that you want to speak	I have a point to raise.
Introducing a topic	'The subject of my presentation is . . .'
	'About those invoices . . .'
Stating purpose	'I want to suggest some solutions.'
	'I'd like to explain the background.'
Stating aims/objectives	'The aim of this report is to . . .'
	'We have two objectives . . .'
Describing the structure of a talk or message	Before I deal with this question, let me just . . .'
Moving to a new point	'Let's move on to the next point'
Postponing	'I'll come back to that later'
Identifying reasons/ problems/results	'The reason is . . .'
	'The problem is . . .'
	'Let me explain what happened'
Introducing a conclusion or summary	'So to conclude . . .'
	'Let's summarize the main points.'

Emphasizing important points

As with organizing the message, some aspects of emphasizing are non-linguistic—for example, identifying the important points and placing them in a prominent position in the text. However, indicating emphasis is a specifically linguistic skill.

Ways to show emphasis when giving information orally:

- Explicit statement ('an important point')
- Use of intensifiers ('really', 'absolutely', 'definitely')
- Word order: ('What is important is . . .', 'It is the cost which is important')
- Use of intonation and stress
- Use of pitch and pausing.

Ways to show emphasis in writing:

- The first three points in the previous list apply to writing as well as speaking, although the words used may belong to a more formal register.

- Word order and sentence structure to show emphasis will be particularly important in writing.
- Punctuation
- Sentence length (short sentences can be very powerful)
- Emphasis can also be shown in writing by means of layout and graphical features (use of bold/underlining).

Telephoning

Telephoning can be distinguished as a performance area even though it actually refers to a channel of communication and may cover a wide range of situations and types of interaction. This is because the language used on the telephone is highly conventional and formalized. Many words and expressions are used only on the telephone, either because they relate to the technology or because of the need for rituals and routines in a difficult communicative situation.

'*It's Bill Smith from London. Do you want to speak to him?*'

Telephoning also requires well-developed skills in exchanging information, clarifying, and explaining. Since the speakers cannot fall back on visual support (graphics, figures, pictures, gestures, facial expressions, or body language), the stress on the spoken word is greater than in any other interactive situation. Table 9.4 lists some of the skills and their related functions and language.

Table 9.4: Skills, functions, and language features relating to telephoning

Skill	Function	Language
getting through	requesting, introducing self, checking identity, stating purpose of call	Vocabulary: caller, dial, exchange, hold the line
		Appropriacy: e.g. 'This is . . .' v. 'I am . . .' 'Is that . . .' v. 'Are you . . .?'
		Politeness: e.g. 'Could I speak to . . .?' v. 'Give me . . .'
taking/leaving messages	offering/asking for information	'Who's calling, please?' v. 'Who's that?'
		Pronunciation: numbers, spelling
making appointments	accepting, declining, confirming	Structural: questions, modals, time prepositions, adverbs, time clauses
exchanging information	clarifying, repeating, rephrasing, requesting, repetition	
making complaints	stating dissatisfaction, apologizing, requesting/demanding/ promising action	
finishing the call	confirming, checking, negotiating end of call, saying goodbye	Stress and intonation

Business correspondence

As with telephoning, there are certain conventions that need to be followed when writing business letters, faxes, or telexes—conventions that are much more rigidly adhered to than the telephoning conventions. A separate checklist of language functions and features is therefore included here (see Table 9.5 overleaf).

Table 9.5: Functions and linguistic skills for business correspondence

Function	Appropriate language
opening and closing the communication	Common abbreviation and conventions: 21/03/94 Attn. C. Kennedy Yr. ref. Dear Sir/Yours faithfully Dear Mr. Jones/Yours sincerely
stating purpose	I am writing to let you know. . .
stating the subject referring to enclosures referring to previous communications	Here is the report you asked for. Please find enclosed the report you requested.
making an enquiry	Would you please let us know Please send. . . We should be most grateful if you would send. . .
thanking	We are very grateful for. . .
apologizing	Please accept our apologies for the delay
expressing dissatisfaction or complaining	We are concerned that. . . Yet again we have to remind you that. . .
promising action	We will give this matter our immediate attention.

Socializing

This performance area is not, of course, exclusive to Business English: in fact, some might say that it does not belong to Business English at all. However, a great many Business English learners feel insecure about the social situations they must deal with and feel it is a necessary component of their course.

What do we mean by socializing? There are three distinct types of situation and behaviour. The first is the transactional situation where the speaker has a particular purpose—for example, ordering a meal in a restaurant. In this situation, there are often set routines, predictable formulae, and fairly predictable time boundaries. Skills for handling these situations will be essential for anyone who travels to other countries, and may be termed 'Survival English'. The second type of situation is where people make contact with others for business reasons but, around the actual discussion of business, will need to carry out certain social rituals in

English—for example, greeting and saying goodbye. The third is where speakers interact with no fixed purpose other than to pass the time of day or to create a more relaxed atmosphere in which they can get to know each other better. This may be termed 'Conversational English'.

Survival English

Table 9.6 identifies areas which are useful for many Business English learners who travel to countries where they will use English to get around.

Table 9.6: Functions and language for 'Survival English'

Situation	Function	Language
Ordering meals in a restaurant, ordering drinks in a bar	Attracting attention requesting, offering, accepting, declining	Politeness: 'Excuse me . . .', 'Please . . .', 'Could I have . . .?', v. 'Give me . . .'
Dealing with taxi drivers, changing money, hiring a car, finding out about times and schedules, asking the way, asking about prices	asking for information thanking, complaining, apologizing	Structural components: questions: direct and indirect, modal verbs Cultural features: e.g. use of Sir Stress and intonation to show politeness

Rituals

Table 9.7: Functions and language in rituals

Function	Language
Greeting people, introducing yourself	Appropriacy of greetings based on familiarity and cultural background
polite enquiries during the first five minutes of a meeting	e.g. 'How do you do?' v. 'Hi. How are you?'
thanking, complimenting, responding to thanks and compliments	Formulae: e.g. 'It's very kind of you.' 'Not at all.'

Small talk between people who do not know each other well is also a ritual and usually comprises very predictable topics and language. Learners can be taught certain language routines involving typical question and answer patterns. Topic routines include:

- the weather
- travel to the place of meeting
- accommodation
- previous visits to a country or town
- topics relating to the visitor's own country or town.

Personal topics are usually avoided at first meetings—or are avoided altogether in some cultures. However, in other cultures it may be common to ask about the family or about health. Questions and answers about these topics are also highly ritualistic. Table 9.7 lists ritual situations in English.

Conversational English

Conversation skills are deeply bound up with culture and personality and are very hard to teach. Conversational interactions have no clear agenda and may leap from topic to topic. Selection of topics can be from shared experience of the past (memories of things people did together) or of the present (weather, surroundings, topical events, etc.). Allusions and references are often deeply rooted in personal relationships and the shared experiences of the people involved. There are also strong cultural features which affect, for example, the role of humour in conversation and the kinds of topics that are considered acceptable. Time boundaries are also a cultural feature affecting the amount of conversation that is expected to take place before, after, or even during a business meeting.

It is difficult to predict the functional areas that might be useful, but learners can be given strategies for raising topics, changing topic, and accepting or rejecting new topics. Listening and reacting will be of utmost importance—for example, picking up on something another person says and turning it into a topic:

> A I don't live in London actually.

> B Oh, where do you live then?

The use of discourse markers such as 'actually', 'then', and 'well' could also be examined and practised.

Aspects of conversation are referred to later in Part Three.

Language analysis

The above breakdown of business performance areas will provide a useful corpus of skills and functions for a wide range of Business English courses. But what happens when the need is more specific? What should the trainer do if confronted with, for example:

- a group of bankers working in a foreign exchange department
- an engineer working in materials handling in the field of telecommunications
- a group of learners who want to follow a computer manual?

How can the trainer arrive at the key functions, structures, and vocabulary which need to be learned? A bottom-up approach is needed whereby samples of actual language used in specific situations are analysed to see what language features should be included in the syllabus. An overall view of how this language analysis step fits in with other analysis procedures is shown in Figure 9.1.

Figure 9.1: Analysis procedures

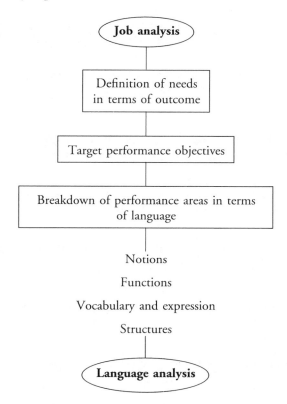

Company documentation

As mentioned in Chapter 8, a useful strategy in preparing for a course is to ask the company for any documents that are typical of those the learners must refer to in their work. These documents could be general (relating to the company as a whole) or specific (relating to the learner's own job). The specific documents will be useful for analysing the kind of language which the learner must acquire either an active or passive knowledge of.

Below are two extracts from such documents, followed by a brief commentary of the kind of language analysis which can be made from them.

Extract from company brochure on distribution of telecommunications products

> *Supplier to customer:* Deliveries from the supplier direct to the customer occur for articles of a high value and a low frequency of use. The orders refer to specific objects with long lead times, for example [named digital exchanges], private branch exchanges and big cables. The aim is combined shipments, but the long lead times give rise to problems both with supplier and customer, which can lead to deliveries in steps. The local stores gather the articles in special transit storerooms pending shipment to customer. Transit storing is however very costly and is therefore avoided.

Analysis

Functions
Defining: what kind of articles are shipped direct to the customer?
Cause and effect: 'long lead times give rise to problems . . . which can lead to deliveries in steps.'
Stating aim: 'The aim is . . .'.
Stating disadvantages: 'Transit storing is however very costly . . .'.

Structures
The use of the present simple for describing what usually happens; use of linking words—'but', 'therefore', 'however'.

Vocabulary
General sales and distribution vocabulary: 'delivery', 'customer', 'supplier', 'articles', 'order', 'high value', 'transit', 'lead time', 'stores', 'shipment', 'costly'.

Telecommunications vocabulary: 'exchanges', 'private branch exchanges', 'cable'.

Extract from a user's manual on electronic mail

> With the Mail Function you can:
> Electronically send letters and documents to an individual or group. You can specify a priority of relative importance (high, low, and so on); a class (first class, registered, or certified); security (private or none); and you can encrypt mail. By using the directory, you can locate users and create a mailing list.

Mailbox—A file which is created by the system in the folder your.dsk. An incoming.mbx [mailbox] file is created when you receive mail. An outgoing.mbx file is created when you file a copy of the mail you send. A phone.mbx file is created when you receive a phone message. A phonelog.mbx is created when you file a copy of the phone message you send.

Encryption—Coding which requires the recipient to use a keyword for decoding so they can open the mail. Further explanation is given in R5-5 (3 of 3), "Fields of the Electronic Mail Screen".

Analysis

Functions
Describing functions (what the user can do) and methods (how to do it):
'By using . . .'.
Defining terminology
Describing what happens
Referring to other parts of the manual

Structures
Modal verbs: 'can'
Present simple passive
Present simple active
Relative clauses
Time clauses

Vocabulary
General office vocabulary: 'letters', 'documents', 'file', 'copy', 'mail', 'phone message', 'priority', 'security', 'list', 'group'.
Specific vocabulary: 'first class', 'registered', 'certified', 'encrypt', 'directory', 'locate', 'create', 'incoming', 'outgoing', 'receive', 'recipient', 'keyword', 'decoding'.

The usefulness of analysing these kinds of documents will vary considerably depending on the learners and their needs. If the group needs to learn how to use a computer manual, the manual itself will form the basis for the course, which will then be highly specific in terms of objectives and content. Such a group is likely to be at a low level in language ability. Thus, the analysis of language in the manual will provide the bulk of the syllabus in terms of function, structure, and vocabulary, most of which is likely to be new for the learners. During the course, the trainer will then focus on developing effective reading skills within the context provided by the manual.

In the case of the telecommunications engineer, the usefulness of the brochure is less clear. The selection of items to be taught will depend on the existing knowledge of the learner, and also on specific skills needs:

whether to understand and follow or to explain the procedure to another person. The language used in the brochure may be a useful reference for the trainer, helping him or her to understand the principles involved and to know the relevant terminology used in describing them. If the learner is relatively low level or has difficulty expressing him or herself, the trainer can refer to the language in the brochure for teaching and learning support. However, it will be important to remember that written language differs greatly from spoken, and if the learner's objectives are to explain procedures orally, then the precise language of the brochure may be inappropriate, and may set false targets for the learner who sees it as a model. (See also Chapter 12 on exploiting authentic material.)

Learner output

A readily available source of material for language analysis in the case of job-experienced learners is the output from the learners themselves. This source is by definition imperfect—probably in terms of structure as well as vocabulary—but the functions are often clearly identifiable, and provide a base for the trainer to deduce the structure and vocabulary needs of the learners.

As before, two extracts are included here with a commentary to show how the analysis can be made.

Extract from a presentation given by an engineer working in materials handling in the telecommunications industry

> We deliver materials different ways to the different store parts, and it depends on what kind of material it is. We also have direct deliveries from the supplier to the customer. It's telephone exchange and big PABX to big customers. But the administration is done by the telecom area, but the deliveries are direct.

> We only make the agreements that we want, for example five big exchanges for next year, and then the local telecom area order it from the suppliers, and directly out to the customers.

> And then we have a special deliveries for telecom and data sales and . . . this kind of equipment is delivered directly from the suppliers to the sales shops, not through the central warehouses.

Analysis
Functions
Defining: what kind of deliveries are made direct to the customer?
Describing procedure: what normally happens, what is done.
Sequencing.

Structures

The use of the present simple for describing what usually happens; and present simple passive. (The learner uses these successfully.)

Use of linking words to show sequence, contrast, and addition: 'but', 'also', 'then'. (The learner needs to develop this area.)

Vocabulary

General sales and distribution vocabulary: 'delivery', 'customer', 'supplier', 'direct', 'order', 'store', 'warehouse', 'agreement'.

Telecommunications vocabulary: 'exchanges', 'PABX'. Some vocabulary usage needs to be clarified and more precise alternatives found or examples given: 'store parts', 'materials', 'telecom and data sales'. Although the learner has a reasonable vocabulary, some work in this area would be useful provided it is clearly directed and challenging.

Extract from a discussion by a group of bankers on the role of the foreign exchange department

A The normal work of the foreign exchange department is to take the risk from the customer into the bank . . .

B Yeh, or . . . prepare some cover, buying forward money and so on, and to take the risk away from the bank as far as the refinancing side is concerned. You could imagine that the bank is granting, grants a loan in US dollars but has no refinancing in that currency.

A But it's not done.

B Okay, but we could think of that.

C It's possible.

B You are absolutely all right, it's the same with the borrowers, that they have their income, let me say, in US dollars—they take a loan in deutschmarks—and suddenly the interest rate increased and they changed the deutschmark loan due to the fact that the Swiss franc was very cheap on the interest level, and then beside that they were affected by three types, first an exchange rate from deutschmarks to Swiss francs exchange, then interest rate in Swiss franc exchange, and also the dollar . . . and this again turns to a credit risk to the bank.

Analysis

It is interesting to note that in this discussion the group do not talk about their department as though they were addressing students, and giving them information. When they talk among themselves they have a common knowledge and common terms of reference which do not need to be explained. It is the language of banking and not the language of the classroom.

Functions
Identifying a problem: the risk that the bank takes when granting a foreign exchange loan.
Describing a sequence of events: as an example of the problem—not to give information about procedures as this is already common knowledge.
Considering possible scenarios: "We could think of that", "It's possible." A more English expression would be: "Let's imagine what happens if . . ." or "what would happen if . . .".

Structures
Speaker B has the choice of the present simple, for describing a possible scenario, or the past for a hypothetical scenario. (In fact he mixes the two tenses.)
Modal verbs for possibility: 'could'.

Vocabulary
Specific terminology: (obviously not a problem for these learners): 'risk', 'cover', 'buying forward', 'refinancing', 'currency', 'granting a loan', 'interest rate', 'credit risk'.
General vocabulary: The use of some words and phrases needs to be clarified: 'You could imagine that . . .', 'but we could think of that', 'You are absolutely all right', 'It's the same with the borrowers', 'let me say', 'beside that', 'they were affected by three types'—the speakers have failed to express the appropriate force and meaning in these examples. This clearly demonstrates that it is not the technical vocabulary which presents a problem for learners at this level of ability, so much as the need to fine-tune meaning and intention.

Observing learner output as a means of analysing language needs can provide many insights for the trainer. It is more accurate and reliable than written documentation in showing what particular learners need to know; however, it is also a considerably more challenging route for the trainers, who have to bring all their resources and knowledge to bear in order to deduce the meaning and translate it into comprehensible English.

Training videos

For trainers working with pre-experience learners, or for those who work mainly with individuals, it may be difficult to find out what sort of language is really being used in business meetings and interactions around the world. One useful source can be business training videos, particularly those designed for work training in a native-speaker environment rather than those designed specifically for language training. Although such videos are scripted, and may lose many aspects of authenticity for the sake of drama, clarity, and the training purpose, they contain many useful examples of the interactive and transactional functions that are common in business.

Extract from the LTS video *Systems One*

The speakers in this extract are brainstorming the causes of a problem concerning a computerized stock control system.

> **A** The stock system does have a safeguard which might have brought this problem to light much earlier, though it wasn't designed with inter depot transfers in mind. But this safeguard was overlooked in operation, and not applied.
>
> **B** What safeguard?
>
> **A** It's a procedure that . . . [explains the procedure]
>
> **B** Now just a minute. I want to be quite clear about this. You keep a record of all inter depot deliveries, and you match that against inter depot receipts, and if they agree you cancel them out. Is that right?
>
> **A** Yes.
>
> **B** And if they don't agree?
>
> **A** There's a monthly printout of all exceptions that haven't been matched.
>
> **B** All cases where details of receipts and deliveries don't agree?
>
> **A** Right. So if warehouse A says it's sent ten items and warehouse B says it's received nine items, there's a mismatch and all the details are printed out.
>
> **B** Then what happens?

(This video was originally published by Melrose under the title *What's so Special about Computers?*—see Appendix.)

Analysis

Functions
Describing procedure
Explaining what did or did not happen
Giving information
Clarifying information
Confirming information.

The most interesting aspect of language in this extract is the different means used by speaker B to check that he has understood:
Direct questions: ('What safeguard?')
Controlling the pace: ('Now just a minute. I want to be quite clear about this.')
Summarizing information given: ('You keep a record of all inter depot deliveries . . . you match that against inter depot receipts . . .')
Check questions: ('Is that right?')
Testing hypothesis: ('And if they don't agree?').

Vocabulary

The vocabulary used in this extract may also be useful if the learners are involved in a similar kind of work. The telecommunications engineer quoted above, for example, might find the content of this video extract useful, as well as the strategies it exemplifies.

Again, this extract demonstrates an interaction in which problem-solving is the main purpose. Information is rarely exchanged for its own sake in a business environment; there is almost always an underlying element of trying to achieve a goal.

The focus of training

This chapter has concentrated on how to determine the areas of language to be taught on a course of Business English, and has identified some of the functions, structures, and vocabulary most likely to be needed. However, it is important to remember that the overall objective of Business English courses is to improve performance. This objective cannot be achieved if the course devotes too much time to input and not enough to output.

Much traditional teaching in Business English has consisted of the handing out of lists of gambits and formulae. Learners have found themselves with long lists of phrases which are supposed to help them to agree, disagree, put forward points of view, or interrupt. Our view is that trainers should treat gambits as only one of several means of achieving certain goals. They are useful as props, although they may not reflect native-speaker use. Some research data shows that native speakers of English can be limited in their use of gambits—see Williams (1988). They do not go around saying 'I disagree completely' or 'I can't go along with that'. They are much more likely to indicate disagreement rather than express it overtly. Native speakers will probably use intonation and pitch rather than fixed expressions to indicate the finer shades of meaning. Whilst many learners will probably be unable to do this effectively themselves, they may need to be aware of this feature.

It may be argued, of course, that learners need to use gambits because they lack proficiency in the use of the subtler means of expression. However, there should be a limit to the amount of stress placed on the teaching of them. First, if the learners are given too many items to learn at the same time, they will be unable to learn all of them and will be confused about differences in their usage. Second, if it is an important objective of an activity to use a newly-learned formulaic phrase, then many other important skills may be overlooked—for example, listening to what other participants in a meeting are saying, or trying to be precise in giving information or expressing the details of an argument.

This chapter has dealt with the problem of selecting the language areas for a course. The question of how the different elements of a course may be put together, balanced, and sequenced is considered in Chapter 13, page 209.

PART THREE

Activities and materials

INTRODUCTION

After the trainer or training organization has thoroughly analysed the needs of the learners and has set precise objectives for the course, the next step is to select the type of materials which will best help the learners to achieve their objectives. The choices made will determine to a large extent what happens during the course. First, the choice of materials determines what kind of language the learners will be exposed to and, as a consequence, the substance of what they will learn in terms of vocabulary, structures, and functions. The range and complexity of this language has to fit in with the learners' needs, existing knowledge, and capacity for learning. Second, the choice of materials has implications for the methods and techniques by which the learners will learn. Third, the subject or content of the materials is an essential component of the package from the point of view of relevance and motivation. Choosing appropriate materials can pose a number of problems for trainers. On the one hand, there is nowadays a great deal of published material for Business English trainers to choose from; on the other hand, it often seems that none of the available material is exactly right for a particular lesson or for a particular learner or group.

Inexperienced trainers or, indeed, experienced but very busy trainers, like to be able to rely on a published coursebook, which makes all the decisions for them in terms of syllabus, content, and methodology. It must be borne in mind, though, that publishers aim to reach the widest possible market. Trying to meet the needs of the majority usually means that only some of the needs of an individual are satisfied: specific needs cannot be addressed. In situations where a group of learners is relatively heterogeneous and the objectives for learning are non-specific, then a published Business English coursebook may well provide an effective core of material for a course, provided that its level and methodology are appropriate. An individual, or a homogeneous group with specific needs, will also require supplementary materials which trainers may wish to develop and tailor to learners' needs themselves.

Part Three examines three approaches to selecting and developing materials for Business English.

Chapter 10 deals with published materials and how to evaluate them. Chapter 11 presents techniques for developing frameworks which access the learners' own knowledge and experience. These techniques will enable trainers to relate to the specific needs of individuals, whether in individual tuition or in a group. Chapter 12 shows how a trainer can make use of authentic material to devise tasks and activities that are specific and relevant to the learner(s). None of these approaches should be taken as the single best solution to the problem of choosing materials. Most trainers will probably find that a combination of the three approaches (in varying proportions) can best meet the wide-ranging needs of the different types of learners they have to deal with.

Finally, Chapter 13 looks at some different aspects of classroom management appropriate to teaching one-to-one and in groups; and at the kinds of activities relevant to each. There is also a short consideration of course design and of the factors involved in balancing the activities on a course.

10 PUBLISHED MATERIALS

This chapter will consider two categories of published materials available to the Business English trainer. The first includes all those materials aimed at the teaching of English in a business context. The second category comprises materials which are aimed at the business skills training market, and which are not specifically designed for the teaching of language, although they can provide a useful vehicle for language training at a more advanced level. The first two sections give a breakdown of each of these categories in order to provide an overview of what is available on the market. The third section looks at criteria for selection and suggests some strategies for evaluating the various options.

Business English materials

When faced with a row of books on a shelf, all purporting to target Business English learners, it is essential to be able to recognize easily the different aims and purposes of each one.

What is the role of books in a Business English course? The following section considers the different roles which a book (or usually a package of book plus cassettes or book plus video) might have.

General business coursebook packages

If the package aims to be a comprehensive course in itself, it will try to deal with all the aspects of language and skills development at the level specified on its cover. Such packages will be based on a syllabus, which could be structural, functional, or situational. The contents list will normally indicate the orientation of the syllabus. (See the examples in Figures 10.1, 10.2, and 10.3.) Although many coursebooks include some material in all of these areas, there is usually a primary focus. Coursebooks aim to provide material for use at each stage of the lesson: in principle, the trainer need never look for materials elsewhere. Some coursebooks have an ongoing story-line which constrains the users to work sequentially through the course. (Video courses are often constructed in this way—for example, the BBC's *Bid for Power.*) Other coursebooks are modular in construction, which gives the trainer the flexibility to select the elements that are felt to be most useful, and in any order that seems appropriate. These general business courses cannot address any job-specific interests (for example, accounting) and usually select business themes that are of interest to a wide audience.

Figure 10.1: Example of a coursebook with a topic and grammar focus

Extracts from the Contents page of *Business Targets* by Simon Greenall (Heinemann Educational Books, 1986)

CONTENTS

Unit one	**Company organisation**	4
Unit two	**Job descriptions**	12
Unit three	**Manufacturing**	20
Unit four	**Finance and accounting**	28
Unit five	**Marketing new products**	36

. . .

STRUCTURE REVIEW	83
Articles and numbers	83
Compound verbs	84
Conditionals	85
Gerunds and infinitives	86

. . .

Figure 10.2: Example of a coursebook with a storyline and functional language focus

Extracts from the contents page of *Functioning in Business* by Knowles, Bailey, and Jillett (Longman, 1991)

CONTENTS

Figure 10.3: Example of a coursebook with a language and skills focus:

Extracts from the contents page of *Business Objectives* by Vicki Hollett (Oxford University Press, 1991)

Contents

1   Meeting People   *page 6*

Objective	Topics	Language	Skills work
to meet overseas contacts and get to know them	Describing jobs Describing responsibilities Describing tasks Personal details Countries and nationalities	Prepositions – jobs Present simple tense *Wh-* question forms	*Writing:* a personal profile *Speaking:* the conference game

. . .

4   Product Description   *page 32*

Objective	Topics	Language	Skills work
to describe a product or service	Description Size and dimension Describing what you need	Adjectives Dimensions *It weighs/costs* . . .	*Speaking 1:* a crossword *Listening:* presenting a new product to the sales team *Speaking 2:* executive toys

Supplementary materials

These can be books or packages consisting of book plus cassette or book plus video. They do not attempt to treat every aspect of language learning, but instead choose to focus on a particular area such as listening, reading, role play, or vocabulary. Some supplementary materials may focus on a particular area of skills: for example, meetings or socializing. It is expected that the trainer will normally use these materials in addition to a general coursebook in order to provide extra practice in a required skill or language area.

A trainer may choose supplementary materials in a different medium from the one used for core teaching—for example, video (if not used with the

core material) or computer-based materials. Supplementary video materials will be arranged in modules, and may be used to practise functional
language or specific business skills, such as presentations. Computer-based
learning packages can be used to present business problems and involve
the learners in discussing and trying out different solutions which are then
analysed by the computer.

Job-specific materials

There are a number of books on the market which aim to provide language practice within a defined job area—for example, banking,
import–export, secretarial, and accountancy. These are not usually intended to develop the general language skills of the learner in a systematic way,
but to provide some of the target language considered to be useful in these
specific fields. They usually cover specialist vocabulary and provide reading or listening practice in a relevant context. They may also include
speaking and/or writing tasks, and functional or structural language practice. It is important to examine the content and methodology of such
books carefully. A book entitled *English for Banking*, for example, may not
necessarily meet the needs of a group of bankers, particularly if the
members of the group already have a lot of work experience.

Reference books

These include specialist dictionaries, and also reference to books which are
designed to be used to look up the answer to a problem or query. There
are dictionaries for Business English in general, or specific ones for such
areas as Banking, Law, Economics, and Computers, which are useful for
the trainer as well as for the learner.

Handbooks or workbooks are aimed mainly at learners, whether or not
they are attending a course. They are often strongly vocabulary-orientated,
but may give explanations of key business language—functional and
structural. Some provide factual information or tips, for example about
how to behave politely or cultural differences. They often provide exercise
material and include a key for those learners working on their own.

Self-access materials

Some packages are designed specifically for the self-access market, and
some are designed to be used either in the classroom or for self-access.

In principle, any book containing exercise material with explicit explanations and keys can be used for self-access. However, the majority of
learners will soon tire of working through endless grammar or vocabulary

exercises if there is no other stimulus to learning. Specially-designed self-access courses aim to make the learning process as stimulating as attending a class would be. These generally involve more than one medium. Cassette courses are useful for workaholic businesspeople who want to make use of the time they spend driving to work, or travelling by train or plane. Video is a more exciting medium, and video learning packages for Business English are becoming increasingly popular. Another field is computer-assisted language learning, which lends itself well to self-access. Many learners nowadays have a personal computer at home, at work, or at their place of study, and there is a growing amount of software available for language learning. One example of a self-access package for Business English presents letter-writing conventions, together with exercises for practising the language. Large companies and educational establishments are now equipped with interactive video, which combines the stimulus of video with the control functions of a computer. This enables the learner to access the answers to questions, an on-line dictionary, and many other learning support functions while watching a specially-prepared video. Interactive video programmes are available for Business English (see Suggestions for Further Viewing in the Appendix).

Business skills training materials

There is a growing amount of business skills training material on the market, mostly aimed at company training programmes and business schools. Although they are not designed for language teaching, and are often considerably more expensive than dedicated language teaching material, there are many good reasons why these materials (carefully selected) can provide a valuable resource for Business English trainers. These materials are created and designed by people with a lot of business and business training experience. The target skills and practices have been carefully researched and the contexts in which the training points are presented have a high credibility. The market is more profitable and production budgets are therefore higher than in the Business English market, and this results in very high-quality products.

Business skills training materials provide a bridge between Business English materials and authentic materials. They are produced for training purposes and they cannot be said to model authentic language. However, the scripting of business training videos usually comes closer to natural English than that of Business English videos. They are valuable for trainers and learners who have not had business experience because they provide insights into typical business situations, behaviours, and procedures. Even job-experienced learners may learn something from them (for example, how to co-operate with others to solve problems, how to negotiate more effectively). But the main objectives in using the material for Business English purposes will be language-related. For example: a business simulation game may provide an excellent opportunity for a group of learners to discuss a business problem in English; a management training video featuring a meeting may be a useful vehicle for introducing key language, together with an opportunity to develop effective listening skills for meetings.

Business skills training materials would normally fill a supplementary role rather than providing the basis for a course.

There are several different kinds of material available, and further information about two main categories, videos and games, is given below. A third category which might be considered is case studies. These are normally developed for management training and present a business case, or problem, which a group of learners must discuss and find solutions for. The main problem in using these with language learners is that they normally involve a great deal of background reading, and often more time may be spent in absorbing the details of the case than in discussing and developing interactive skills. They are also difficult to obtain as they are usually produced by management training schools and are not generally sold to the public. Some Business English materials present case studies which are much more manageable in terms of the amount of background data provided, and the level of language used to present the data. Depending on the needs of a particular group, it will probably be advisable to opt for these rather than actual management training case studies.

Video materials

These videos may focus on various themes: general business skills (for example, how to run effective meetings, how to sell, how to structure a presentation); personal development skills (for example, how to deal with awkward customers, team-building, how to be a good boss); good business practice (for example, project management, finance control, data security).

Some videos take a serious approach to the presentation of the main training points, perhaps using a presenter to explain and short scenes of critical incidents to illustrate. An example of this type is the video *Going International*, which gives advice to Americans doing business internationally who could meet difficulties because of a lack of cross-cultural awareness. Others use a humorous style of presentation, often involving a somewhat comic character who does everything wrong. The Video Arts series of training videos has many examples of this type. Others may use drama: a serious situation develops in a company which could have been avoided if the people responsible had been aware of certain important business strategies. Examples of this type can be found in the Melrose series of training films (see the Appendix for a list). All are entertaining to some degree, although in the case of humorous videos especially, the trainer must consider to what extent the style of presentation is suitable for his or her learners.

Before using a business skills video, the trainer should think carefully about the best way to exploit it from a language learning perspective. Some videos can be purchased as a package including ready-made language teaching materials. (See Appendix for a list.) Alternatively, the school may have developed its own materials for use with the videos in its library. Ideas for exploiting video materials are given in Chapter 12, page 169.

Business simulation games

These can be categorized in two main groups: in-context games and out-of-context games. In-context means that the game simulates real life as nearly as possible. This group includes sales and negotiation role plays, problem-solving discussions, or simulated meetings set in a modern business environment. Out-of-context games are those which practise the target skills in unreal or unlikely situations. Games in this group may require the participants to imagine that they are on the moon or living in Ancient Egypt at the time of the Pharaohs.

Games are designed to train businesspeople in interpersonal skills, for example, co-operation, listening, leadership. Apart from those that have a specified target audience (for example, sales role-plays are for sales representatives), they can usually be used with a wide range of people. The main requirement is that the language ability of non-native speakers should be high enough to enable them to participate. One of the principal values of these games is that the participants become so involved that they forget their fear of speaking English: they gain considerable fluency practice, and learn to interact and communicate with their fellow learners. Certain language areas can also be targeted by the trainer, such as questioning, clarifying, suggesting, agreeing, and disagreeing. (A list of sources for business skills training materials is given in the Appendix.)

Selection and evaluation

The selection of materials can be made at two levels. First, at the start of a course, the trainer or training organization will probably want to make some decisions about the coursebooks and supplementary materials that will provide the core of material to be used (unless the organization has developed its own materials). Exceptions would be highly specific courses which would need materials to be developed specially, or one-to-one courses for which a more flexible approach is needed. Second, the trainer will need to make decisions about items of material to use for a particular lesson. In both cases, the same factors will affect the trainer's decision; but in the first case, the criteria for selection must somehow apply to a whole book, whereas in the second case, they need only apply to a particular exercise or activity.

As already discussed, a major factor in selecting a book is whether the book can fulfil the role required of it as coursebook, supplementary material, etc. Other criteria which can apply whether one is selecting a book or just one item of material for a lesson; these are considered below.

Criteria for selection

What kind of learner is the material to be used with?

Pre-experience learners have different requirements from job-experienced learners, as we have already seen. Pre-experience learners will still be learning about both the theory and practice of business: the materials most suitable for these learners should therefore provide more information about the subject in question. Materials suitable for job-experienced learners, on the other hand, should assume a background knowledge of business. They should provide language input rather than business input, and should set tasks which require the users to refer to their own experience: for example, 'describe your company's products to a partner'.

The work area and type of job that the learners have, or will have in the future, will also determine what kind of materials will be most relevant. A lot of materials have been developed specially for secretarial and clerical jobs, and these will be very different, in terms of the language and skills areas covered, from materials which are aimed at learners in managerial jobs. When looking for materials in a specific job area, it is important to consider the level and knowledge of the job that the learners already have and what they need to develop. Export managers do not need to concern themselves with the details of completing export documentation, for example; and senior bank staff do not need to be informed about how foreign payments are made because they will know this already. When selecting materials for a specific job area (either a present or a future job), the trainer should look for tasks and activities that practise the target skills areas: meetings, telephoning, or letter-writing, for example. It is not enough simply to present material with an appropriate topic focus; the skills focus is at least as important.

The language level of the learners will be a further factor: whilst general business materials exist at all levels, it is often difficult to match job-specific requirements with language level requirements. However, it is possible to use some materials at a different level from the one they were originally intended for. If the materials contain target language such as vocabulary, it may be possible to simplify or omit some of the tasks used in the materials. An imaginative trainer will be able to devise new tasks that exploit the useful aspects of job-specific material at a level more suited to the learners.

The age and cultural background of the learners must also be taken into consideration. Different types of activity are likely to appeal to different age groups: for example, games and imaginative activities will probably attract young learners more. The use of pictures and colour in a book can indicate the audience for which it is intended: older and more serious learners could be put off by a book that contains strip cartoons or over-bright colours. Trainers should also be familiar with the cultural preferences and taboos of the region where they are working. Ways in which women are portrayed in video material could prove offensive: some cultures may disapprove of women shown wearing mini-skirts; others (such as Scandinavian countries) may take offence if the women are seen to be in subordinate roles being patronized by men. Publishers nowadays do take account of such factors, either by aiming materials at a specified geographical region, or by producing very neutral material that cannot offend anybody. It is, nevertheless, important to be on the look-out for details that could raise objections.

Another factor to consider is what methodology or style will be appropriate for the learners. Learners coming from an education system in which teachers are powerful and facts have to be learned by rote may not readily accept open-ended activities not directly controlled by the trainer. Conversely, learners who have become used to a practical approach may not be able to cope with learning grammar rules. These are extreme cases, but in any learning situation it is useful to consider what kind of activities will be successful with a particular group. Preferences for a particular approach to learning may stem from the educational background, cultural background, or age; or they could be individual preferences. Every group has its own dynamic and the mix of personalities can affect what kind of activities will be successful or unsuccessful. The trainer should experiment to find out what is the best approach to use with a particular group and then select activities accordingly.

What are the training objectives?

As already stressed above, the trainer must select materials which reflect the skills and content needs of the learners at an appropriate language level. For a particular lesson, the trainer should also have in mind the target language area which he or she has chosen to focus on and, if selecting materials from different sources, must consider the role which such materials need to play in the training process. Are materials needed which present the target language in a convenient summary which learners can later refer back to (i.e. as a resource for the learners)? Is there a need for material which demonstrates how language can be used, for example, by means of an audio or video dialogue, or written text? Is the need rather for practising the language in a controlled way? Or do the learners need a vehicle for transferring their passive knowledge into active use, perhaps by means of open pairwork practice, role-play, or simulation? Or perhaps the need is to check what the learners already know, or to test that they remember something already studied. Materials for checking and testing knowledge will be different from those used to develop and practise knowledge. At different times, the trainer will need all these kinds of material. It is therefore important to be able to recognize what a particular piece of material sets out to do.

Materials that will motivate the learner

A piece of material that meets the training objective and all the criteria relating to the learner or group of learners may still be inadequate if it fails to motivate the learner. It is therefore useful to consider what factors might attract or put off the users.

Credibility   Materials designed for Business English and aimed at learners who have some knowledge of the subject must be seen to represent the world that those learners are familiar with. It is unfortunate that many Business English materials have been written by people who do not have enough knowledge about that world. This may be difficult for the less experienced trainer to recognize. However, feedback from the learners will soon indicate what they find acceptable or not.

Up-to-date materials   Some Business English books have been on the market for many years and though they may still contain a lot of useful language input and practice, some aspects of their content now appear dated. The trainer may decide to omit some exercises if they deal with outmoded practice or present old-fashioned ideas or, especially, old-fashioned language.

Attractive materials   However good a piece of material is from a teaching point of view, it may be unacceptable if the presentation is poor—for example, if the layout is cramped, the pictures are difficult to make out, or the tasks are difficult to follow. Business people in developed countries, in particular, are used to a very high standard of presentation and may be put off by poor quality. If there is a choice, therefore, it is better to opt for materials with attractive layout, good visuals, and easy access for the learner. When evaluating audio and video tapes, it is important to choose those which are well-acted and sound reasonably natural. Video materials should look professional and the sound quality must be excellent.

Table 10.1: Checklist for evaluating published materials

1 What kind of learner is the material aimed at?
   − work area
   − work experience
   − language level
   − cultural background
   − educational background
   − age
   − learning style.

2 What are the main language objectives?
   − skills
   − functions
   − structures
   − vocabulary.

3 What are the main topic areas covered?
   − does the material introduce the subject?
   − does it use the topic area as contextual background?
   − is the coverage of the topic content high in credibility?

4 What is the main methodological approach?
   − demonstration of language in context through text, tape, or video
   − explanations of grammatical rules
   − presentation of functional language
   − presentation of vocabulary
   − controlled practice of language
   − open practice of language
   − skills development
      or a combination of these?

5 What is the role of the material?
   − to present language
   − to practise language
   − to provide a resource for the learner
   − to check or test knowledge.

6 Is the material attractive?
- clear layout
- good use of space
- useful, clear pictures and diagrams
- interesting context and tasks.

11 FRAMEWORK MATERIALS

Traditionally, language teaching materials have presented teaching points, structures, vocabulary, or points which relate to the development of particular skills, either as straightforward exercises, or within the context of a narrative or situational written or listening text. However, for some time now many Business English trainers have been looking for ways of giving learners materials that allow *them* to provide the context from their own experience.

This direct use of the learner's personal experience is very important when teaching professionals. Such learners are used to holding down responsible jobs, and performing well and efficiently. When learning English they can feel extremely inadequate. Since the early 1980s, framework materials have been developed as a means of avoiding this demotivating situation. Some of the types of framework presented in this chapter allow the learner to produce content and context which is directly applicable to him- or herself. Even though the language might be poor, the task itself is seen to have value. In this chapter, we discuss examples of materials which encourage the learner to describe contrasts and similarities, to talk about advantages and disadvantages, and to describe cause and effect. These very basic conceptual activities are fundamental to language activity. The framework allows the learner to perform this activity, using a context which has not been chosen by the trainer, while at the same time engaging in real language tasks. Frameworks are designed to be motivating and relevant.

What are framework materials?

Frameworks are usually diagrammatic representations which can be used to generate language. Some represent concepts—for example, the frameworks for describing cause and effect (page 140); others encourage interaction. Some frameworks can be used to guide learners in expressing ideas, giving short explanations or talks or describing situations. Frameworks can be used by pairs or groups of learners to build dialogues and conversations, and organize meetings.

Often, when students make language mistakes, these are the result of poor organization. When the organizational problem is removed, the mistakes either disappear or are minimized. Framework materials actively encourage the user to organize his or her thoughts and language: it can therefore be assumed that any mistakes are more likely to be language mistakes, and not due to problems of organization.

Frameworks are designed to prompt the production of language: they do not present language. Some frameworks may be constructed to practise a grammatical point, such as conditionals; some may practise functional language such as making an invitation and accepting or refusing an invitation. However, the framework does not prescribe exactly what words or expressions the learner should use to carry out the task.

Advantages

1 Low input: high output
Frameworks are easy for a trainer to produce. They can be drawn on the board, or they can be drawn on a sheet of paper or on cards for handing out to learners. There are usually few or no words involved.

At the same time, frameworks can generate a great deal of language practice. Sometimes a single framework can be used as a basis for an extended activity; sometimes, several frameworks can be used together to practise a particular language area in different ways.

2 Focus on organization and discourse
Because frameworks do not dictate precisely which language the learners should use (particular vocabulary items or grammatical structures, for example), they help the learner to focus on the message to be conveyed. The framework enables the learner to organize ideas and to build up discourse according to logical and well-established sequences.

3 Frameworks as a diagnostic and teaching tool
Used at the diagnostic level, frameworks enable the trainer to listen and analyse the weaknesses in the learner's use of language. This might be sentence structure, or how extended speech is handled—the use of the sound system, the use of linking words, the consistency of tense and vocabulary. Once the teaching areas have been identified and the structures or other language focuses demonstrated, framework materials can again be used for practice.

4 At different levels of ability

Because frameworks do not prescribe the language to be used, in many cases the same framework can be used equally effectively with both low-level and high-level learners. A low-level learner would be expected to express an idea using simple constructions within a limited vocabulary range; a high-level learner can express the same conceptual idea but with a much greater range of expression and complexity of language.

Framework materials are also useful in mixed-ability classes, because each learner can be given a task appropriate to his or her level of ability.

5 For learners with different interests

Because framework materials generally do not present a context, they enable the learners themselves to choose a context in which to practise the desired language. This is particularly encouraged through the use of the setting box, which is explained in detail on page 142. The frameworks for describing cause and effect, for example, can be used equally effectively with economists, marketing managers, environmentalists, or psychologists. They have the effect of personalizing the task.

Because learners can use frameworks to talk about the things that interest them, they will be highly motivated and will find the language practice more relevant to their own needs.

6 Modifying the materials

A framework is essentially a tool to be used, and can be modified to meet the needs of an individual or group. For example, the cause–effect framework (14) on page 141 could be modified so that there are two causes and one effect.

When should framework materials be used?

These materials are not a replacement for other types of materials which are available to trainers. They do no more than add an extra dimension to what is already on the market. When deciding on whether to use a framework or not, two main questions need to be asked. The first concerns the trainer: is he or she happy to use material which does not set out to present language, but which, apart from its organizational function, is there to show what the learner can do with language? The second concerns the learners: do they work in a visual way? Learners who are very visual in their learning styles may well find them more appealing and useful than those who are not.

Finally, it must be stressed that framework materials are not a final solution to the trainer's endless quest for good materials. They should be used wisely. Some learners might be at too low a level for certain activities. For example, the setting box (page 142) might be too complex for some groups of students. Also, trainers who deal with low-level learners should not be put off by the high level of communication demonstrated by the two learners discussing their setting box on page 143. Realistically, this is probably not the right kind of task for learners at a low level.

Frameworks for different purposes

Analysing

Framework 1

This task helps explain where the important lines of communication are in any individual learner's work situation. Like other analysing frameworks it is also a chance to check the learner's use of spoken English.

Explain that you would like the learner (A) to talk in English about his or her contacts within the company, or with subsidiary companies: at a higher level (B), at a lower level (C), and then on the same level (D and E). At an elementary level, only the bare minimum information need be obtained. With more advanced learners, the trainer might also expect to

Framework 1: Points of contact in the company/organization

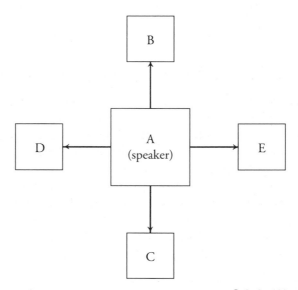

learn more about the reasons for contact, what kind of topics are discussed, how often and where these contacts take place. Points to listen for include individual language errors, the ways in which the speaker starts, the movement from one box to another, and how the set of four is finally included.

Framework 2

This task helps find out more about those who attend meetings.

Framework 2

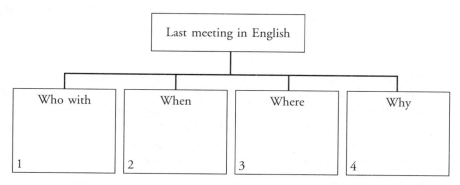

© Oxford University Press 1994

Framework 3

This task is useful in analysing individual language levels and habits at the very beginning of a course. After analysis, the trainer can work towards negotiating individual and group language objectives for the course. In this example the group is a marketing group. Each learner chooses one of the topics below and is given a short time to prepare a three-minute presentation. Marketing people are familiar with presentations and they should only need 30 seconds or so to orientate themselves. Tell the learners to relate the topic to a product with which they are familiar.

- ingredients
- packaging
- current trends
- advertising
- outlets
- pricing.

Exactly the same task, but with different topics, can be prepared for a wide range of business functions, industry sectors, and professions.

Describing contrast and similarity

Frameworks 4–8

In the following frameworks the diagrams have these meanings:

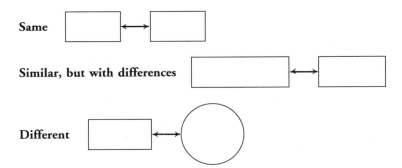

Same

Similar, but with differences

Different

These visual reflections of sameness and difference can be used to practise the language of contrast and similarity. This involves grammatical forms (*-er* forms, 'less', 'more', 'as . . . as', etc.) and specific linking words ('on the other hand', 'in contrast', etc.). Sameness and difference can also be expressed in other ways altogether, simply through the statement of fact— 'Company X produces cars. Company Y produces trucks.'

An example of these five types can be seen in this sample controlled exercise below:

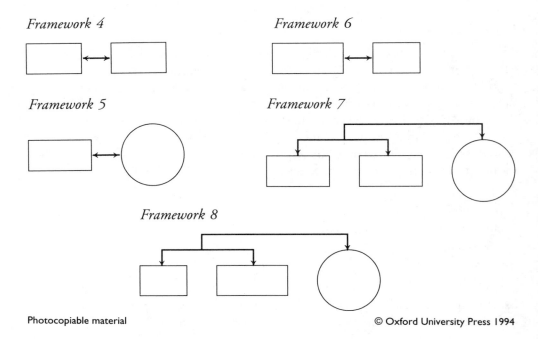

Framework 4

Framework 6

Framework 5

Framework 7

Framework 8

Describe the similarities and differences of the three countries, A, B, and C below:

	A	**B**	**C**
Framework 4	Produces coal	Produces coal	
Framework 5	Produces poor quality coal	Produces high quality coal	
Framework 6	Produces coal		Does not produce coal
Framework 7	Produces coal	Produces coal	Does not produce coal
Framework 8	Produces poor quality coal	Produces high quality coal	Does not produce coal

The examples below are of learners working on the type of comparison in Framework 8, first before being shown the framework diagram. The second set of examples are after looking at the diagram. The learners were instructed first to show that although A and B are similar, there are also some differences, but that country C is completely different.

Learner 1
Before

'We have one country has high quality coal. And one country has low quality coal. And one country hasn't coal.'

After

'We have three countries. Two of them has coal. The third hasn't any coal. The two country have coal, one of them has high quality coal, the other has low quality.'

Learner 2
Before

'While the coal of country A is higher quality than country B's coal, country C doesn't produce any coal.'

After

'Although country A and B both produce coal, in country A the quality is higher. Country C doesn't produce any coal.'

Commentary

The second learner is at a higher level than the first. In their first attempt, both learners failed to identify immediately that A and B produce coal. This is remedied in the second attempt as they had focused on showing the similarity. Also, the attempt to show that there is, however, a difference between A and B is better stated in the second attempt. Again, in the second attempt the contrast with country C is much more clearly stated. Although it could be argued that more work on clarifying the organization could be done, after the second attempt the trainer's focus with learner 1 is much more on grammatical features, such as agreement. The second learner has produced clear and correct English. Later in the course, the first learner went on to make a contrast along the lines of that in Framework 8 about his own industry sector: 'Car-maker Suzuki produces small off-road cars, while Rover produces bigger off-road cars. In contrast, Volkswagen doesn't produce any off-road cars.'

Frameworks for comparison and contrast can also be devised to show membership of sets, with varying degrees of sameness and difference, and trainers might develop quite complex structures to show these relationships. But at a very simple level the following example shows how a basic framework can form the basis for a complex presentation on the similarities between products or processes, or how one product, or process, is different from another.

Frameworks 9–11

Frameworks 9, 10, and 11 are for comparison and contrast—for example, where several elements of a product or system or process are being compared with another. It is also possible to use these frameworks to describe advantages and disadvantages.

Framework 9   *Framework 10*

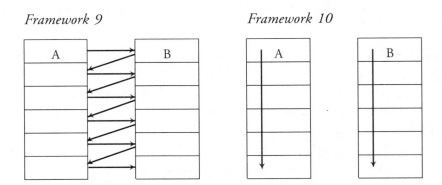

© Oxford University Press 1994

Framework 11

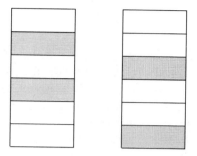

In Framework 9, the speaker is asked to go from A to B step by step, showing the similarities and differences. In Framework 10 all of the points in A are covered first, before moving on to B. In Framework 11 only the main points are highlighted and compared.

The extract below is from a learner who had been instructed to follow Framework 9 in his description of two pick-up trucks, A and B. When he is describing A, he makes reference to a prototype, X.

> I have some general statements for the comparison of A and B, and next I have some specific datas in comparison. Both cars are pick-ups, and they are light pick-ups. A has the basis of the X, and especially the 4-door X. There are many things from the X, the doors, the engine. This [the student points at B] is a truck. A original truck. It has a own driver frame chassis, and an load area. It's a truck. This [pointing at A] is a car. This car is about 17 yeas old and it was developed in USA, in contrast to the, this truck was developed in Japan, from Toyota, and it is, it was batched engineered for us, with a little changes in the front end for the engine, it's our engine, no it's a Japanese engine. This car is built, was built at Sarajevo, and this one is built at Hannover . . .

Commentary

This extract from a presentation clearly shows the learner moving from one pick-up to another, with clear reference to different points of comparison (the origin, the chassis, the engine, the factory). The trainer can focus more on the language than the organization (the use of articles, for example, and though not evident here, the sound system).

Describing change

Framework 12

In this framework the two boxes represent the change that has taken place in a single product (it could also be a process). Box A is as it was. Box B is as it is. (Or, box A is as it is and box B is as it will be.) In this framework we are not looking so much at change from one product to another, but more at product development and improvement. Analysis and correction is likely to focus on how the speaker expresses differences in time.

Framework 12

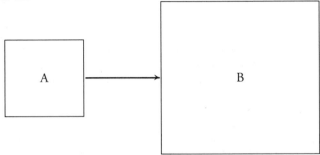

Alternatives

- Focus attention on the cause of the change or the reason for the change
- and/or focus attention on the benefits
- or focus attention on problems which have arisen as a result of the change.

Describing cause and effect

As with other frameworks, these can be used to identify difficulties people have in expressing cause–effect relationships, or identify a limited means of expressing them. They can equally be used to practise what has been input at an earlier stage.

Framework 13

Describe a cause–effect relationship in your own department or company.

Framework 13

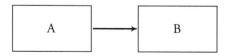

Framework 14

Describe a cause–effect relationship in your work where a single cause can produce two or more effects.

Framework 14

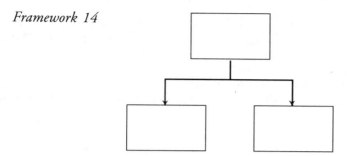

Framework 15

Describe a 'vicious circle' which can exist in your work. Follow the framework, starting in box A.

Framework 15

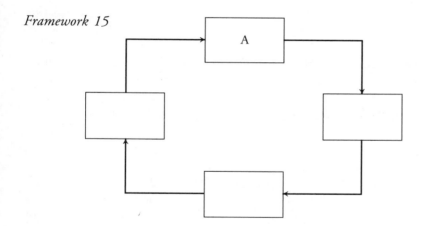

Describing sequence

Framework 16

A simple sequence is just a string of events, joined by linking words such as 'next' and 'then', or 'after' and 'when'-type clauses.

However, it is possible to focus attention on the objective of the sequence, for example, or on one particular stage. In this sequence the learner is asked to highlight the objective and, when mentioning the different stages, to focus on one stage which can prove problematic.

Example: 'The objective of this sequence is to put in place a new system, computer system, for all the water industry. Maybe in twenty sites. And the first stage is . . .'

Other examples can be used when more than one thing is happening—for example, in critical path analysis—and are particularly useful for those working on projects.

Framework 16

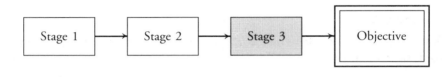

Photocopiable material   © Oxford University Press 1994

By drawing attention to the objective in this way, the speaker starts out on the right foot, leaving the trainer to focus on language instead of organization (for example, interference from the mother tongue ('put in place' instead of 'install' or 'set up'), prepositions, the sound system).

The setting box

One of the great problems for the language trainer is to create enough recognizable context in the language classroom for the learners to produce exchanges which are relevant, and which are not hampered by lack of authenticity, embarrassment, and sheer lack of something meaningful to say.

The setting box is an attempt to overcome this problem. It asks the trainer and the learners to create sufficient context for the task to be meaningful. Before the learners start a dialogue, the setting box asks them to decide who they are, where they are, what they are going to talk about, who with, and why. It asks them to think of where they are, and so to refer to the physical environment (for example, the company office, the fact that it's raining). It asks them to think of what they want to achieve, what their business objectives for this specific language exchange are, and what their immediate communicative objectives are (for example, asking for clarification or evading a question).

Framework 17

In the following example, the setting box is for making recommendations.

The learners complete the setting box. They do this through discussion.

Framework 17

Task	Making recommendations
Who am I? (A)	
Who am I? (B)	
Where are we?	
What are we talking about?	
Why are we talking about this?	

In all of these frameworks, where certain grammatical structures, or particular phrases or words, are used to indicate such relationships as cause or effect, it is very much up to the trainer to decide what to focus on. When analysing rather than actually practising how to show cause–effect, the trainer should listen to see what language is produced rather than instructing the learner to use a particular form.

The following is an example of two learners preparing their setting box. It is noteworthy that one of the learners actually identifies what they are doing and sees the value of it. 'Ah, I see. Now this [heavily emphasized, and referring to their discussion] gives us a good scenario. When you have these targets. Yes.'

Background This activity took place in the second week of a group course. One student is Hungarian (A), the other German (B). The context between them is highly developed. The Hungarian is very aware of the German's interest in cameras.

> A OK, let us say we are in a camera shop. You come to me and I
> make a statement. I don't want to buy . . .
> B You don't want to buy a . . .
> A I don't want to buy a . . .
> B It's too expensive.
> A No, not because it's er, too expensive, but . . .
> B Too complicated?
> A Too much electronics. Like a computer.
> B And so my recommendation is . . .
> A Which camera, is recommend me which is top quality, but which
> is not top features, those electronics . . .

B OK, so you like to have quality but not many features . . .

A Many features. I would like to, I would like to choose the kind, the brand . . .

B Ah, not automatic, but manual . . .

A Other features . . .

B I see . . .

A For example, built-in flash . . .

B Built-in flash?

A Yes.

B Date-maker . . .

A Erm?

B The date on the . . . OK, so I recommend you a special model . . .

A Oh, and I would like to bought a . . .

B To buy . . .

A To buy a six by six. And a second one?

B A second one?

A Yes, maybe a small one.

B Ah, I see. Now this gives us a good scenario. When you have these targets. Yes.

A Well, I think you start. I answer. So, we are ready.

T You are ready?

A, B Yes.

T Could you briefly explain who you are and where you are and what you're talking about?

B Our scenario is in camera shop. He's the customer, client, coming in, stepping in, and I'm the, how do you call it, the seller, the salesperson. He has the special idea and I give him the recommendation.

This preparation itself has already provided valuable language practice. The subsequent role play, involving making a recommendation, is set out below.

B Good morning.

A Good morning. I would like to have some cameras. I have a special idea. I would like to make photos, about buildings and nature, but first I would like to be sure that I find the perfect skene [scene].

B Skene? What is skene?

A Objective. For, er . . . my position . . . so, I would like to have maybe a polaroid so I could have immediate feedback. And then a professional six by six camera which I can make the real picture with.

B OK, so I will try to summarize your idea to find out if I did understand well what your wishes were. And you need one camera with a high quality, six by six, and another one as a polaroid type, to first, and and to use them both together, to first make a shot by polaroid, and then to make another one for a high quality result.

A Yes.

B So, my recommendation would be to take only one camera to save money, and to take a, let's say a Haselbladt six by six, and to buy a polaroid back.

A Mmm. How does it work.

B Well, you can . . .

A I never met . . .

B You can take off the normal back and er put the polaroid back on, make a first shot for polaroid picture, look at it and decide as if whether the quality is good, and then make another shot on the real film.

Commentary

This task, using the setting box, has produced a rich and recognizable language exchange, placing the recommendation at the centre of a web of other communicative purposes. This is in stark contrast to the functional teaching of gambits (formulaic phrases, such as 'If I were you I'd . . .' and 'My recommendation is . . .)'. It illustrates the way frameworking attempts to access the resources available to all learners of English.

Framework 18

The following setting box can be used in a wide variety of circumstances, both for individual learners and for exchanges between learners.

Framework 18

Who am I?
What am I talking about?
Where am I?
Who are my audience?

Framework 19

1 In this case only one learner finishes the setting box.

Use the framework below. Start off speaking, imagining you are addressing an audience. This part is in box A. Then stop and check with a member of the audience (the trainer) to see if the message is getting across. Finally, in box C, continue.

Alternatives are to use box B for other tasks, such as restatement, or giving an example.

Framework 19

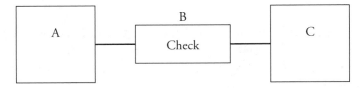

2 For two learners, using the same setting box as in (1) above. B has to evade, or show surprise, interrupt and ask for clarification, interrupt and make a comment, or interrupt and disagree.

In each of these cases the setting box will have been talked through in detail first, in order to create enough context for the task.

For meetings and discussions

Framework 20

This framework is suitable for learners from a similar job background, or from the same company. The framework practises the language of alternative opinions and balancing viewpoints, but in particular it practises listening.

Learner 1 makes a statement about the company (strategy, plans, products, etc.), then chooses a second learner and asks for his or her support.

Learner 2 is unable to support Learner 1, and makes an alternative comment, giving a reason. Learner 2 then asks a third learner for support.

Learner 3 sees good reason to support Learner 1, then asks Learner 4 for support.

Learner 4 sees good reason to support Learner 2 and asks Learner 5 for support.

Learner 5 sees good arguments for both Learners 1 and 2, and goes back to Learner 1 for a comment, or moves on to Learner 6.

Framework 20

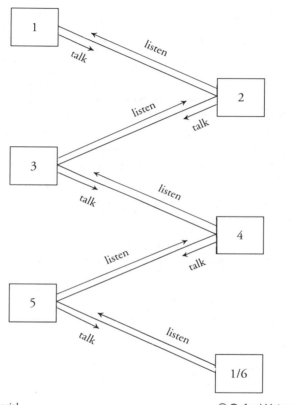

© Oxford University Press 1994

Framework 21: extended meetings

Set-up   This framework is for a group of learners, probably from the same company, and preferably from similar backgrounds. This would allow them to talk about product development, marketing, strategy, for example.

Alternative 1: stages 1–3 only.
Alternative 2: stages 1–4.

Tell the learners that they will be discussing and comparing possible future product development, and that they should follow the procedure outlined in the framework. Tell them that the objective of the exercise is to analyse:

- Individual errors, according to the individual objectives set out beforehand (at the start of the course, during discussion with the trainer, etc.)
- Ability to communicate effectively, in terms of controlling language development, use of intonation and pitch, and projection
- Meetings skills, such as ability to interact, put forward points of view, suggest, balance arguments, lead the meeting forward.

Other words can be substituted for 'product', such as 'company strategy', 'department strategy', 'concerning . . .', 'procedures'.

Stage 1 Divide into teams and in those teams decide on the type of product you wish to develop. Boxes A, B, and C represent different characteristics of the product. Each team should follow Alternatives 1 and 2, discussing two different developments for their product. The characteristics of the product—which might be, for example, positioning, price, customer benefit—are decided now. However, there is no discussion about the merits of the characteristics in Stage 1.

Stage 2 Discuss the comparative characteristics, comparing their merits—for example, the customer benefit of alternative 1 as compared with the customer benefit of alternative 2.

Stage 3 Come to a decision about the product. Choose the best alternatives from each path and be prepared to present a profile of your product in Stage 4.

Stage 4 Meet with the other groups, and together hold a meeting to compare your final products. This may be formal or informal.

Framework 21

Stage 1

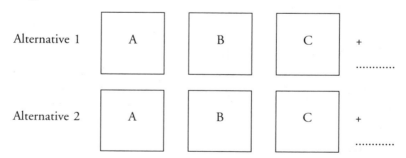

Stage 2

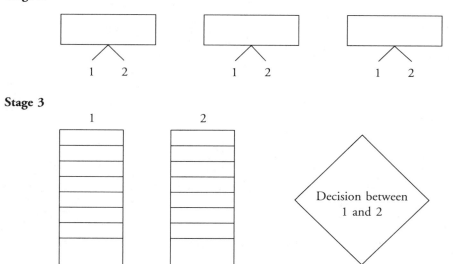

Stage 3

Framework 22: meetings with participants from mixed business backgrounds

Explain that there is going to be a discussion. This will be in two parts. The first is a brainstorming session; the second the discussion itself.

Follow the framework.

Stage 1 Brainstorm a series of topics of general interest which you would be prepared to discuss. One person should control the procedure, writing down each suggestion as it is made. No suggestions should be challenged at this stage. There is no discussion until this stage is over.

Stage 2 Evaluate the suggestions as a group, eliminating the obvious, and ending up with a short list. Select one from the short list.

Stage 3 Create an agenda for your meeting. Do this in the same way as the brainstorming of the topic.

Stage 4 Run the meeting.

Framework 22

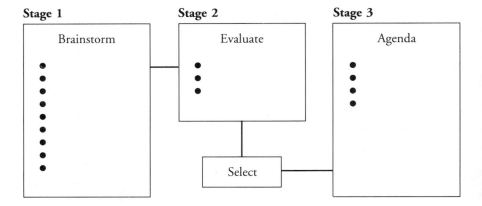

A customer–supplier simulation

Framework 23

This is obviously targeted specifically at those who have this kind of working relationship. Many business problems can arise with this kind of framework, and the trainer should allow the class to discuss their positions in detail. Remind the class of objectives concerning negotiation and/or language skills (already agreed with individuals in the group).

Learners follow the instructions, bearing in mind that two separate discussions are taking place, which in this procedure will run with the teams switching roles between customer/supplier.

Alternatively, Team A can prepare before the activity. The 'Team A as customers' simulation is then played out in its entirety first.

(Adapted from Pilbeam 1991)

Framework 23

Stage	Team A	Team B
1	**Act as customers** Discuss together and decide on a problem/complaint/request to put to the other team	**Act as customers** Discuss together and decide on a problem/complaint/request to put to the other team

2

Act as **customers**	Act as **suppliers**
Present their problem to the other team by letter/telephone/face-to-face meeting	

3

Act as **suppliers**	Act as **customers**
	Present their problem to the other team by letter/telephone/face-to-face meeting

4

Act as **suppliers**	Act as **suppliers**
Discuss solution to the other team's problem	Discuss solution to the other team's problem

5

Act as **customers**   Act as **suppliers**

Teams meet. B present their proposed solution to A. Follow-up discussion in which both teams take part.

6

Act as **suppliers**   Act as **customers**

Teams meet. A present their proposed solution to B. Follow-up discussion in which both teams take part.

Describing production processes

Framework 24

This is one of several framework-type activities that appears in the *Business English Teacher's Resource Book* (Nolan and Reed 1992) and is a further representative of activities which access learners' professional experience with a minimal amount of input on the page. The framework can be used for a group or an individual. The learner(s) brainstorm products which are produced using industrial processes. One product is chosen, box 1 is filled in, and the learner(s) decide what is needed in order to make the product. The learner(s) are then asked to prepare a production process flowchart, using box 2. The product and process are then presented.

Framework 24

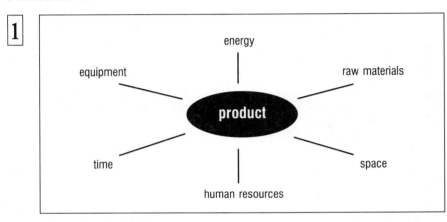

Problem-solving

Framework 25

Explain that this framework practises the language of advantage and disadvantage by showing two different solutions to a particular problem, and why one of them is better than another. In this example, each solution has advantages and disadvantages. The framework is of particular use to those who deal with procedures which involve problem-solving.

Framework 25

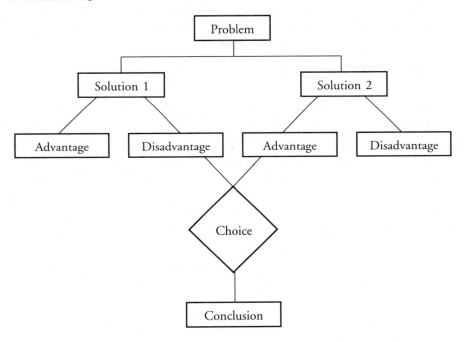

Conversation

Framework 26

When creating role plays for conversations, learners should not be told what to say. However, they must be given enough context for conversation to become possible.

In conversation there is no pre-set agenda—compared with social survival exchanges (for example, in a restaurant, booking a room) where the agenda is explicit.

The setting box for conversations allows the trainer to build up three kinds of time. The first is present time, which refers to everything that is going on at the moment. This includes the physical environment, the people in the room and what they are doing and wearing, the weather, the state of the company, and the current political climate. Present time is shared. Everyone knows all the details. The second kind of time is peripheral time, which again is shared. Peripheral time is time in the past and what can be expected in the future (for example, the people in the conversation below know that there is going to be a meeting). The third kind of time is not shared. This is personal time, which is different for each person. Personal time includes individual constraints and worries, individual beliefs, and individual activities. Personal time, being different for each person in the conversation, provides the information gap so vital to idle enquiry—'So, what did you do last night?'

When setting up conversation practice, explain that as a trainer you will be concentrating on some of these aspects of conversation:

– opening conversations (naming a topic to talk about)
– developing topics (accepting the topic)
– changing topics
– turn-taking (listening, interrupting, guiding)
– negotiating topics (finding a suitable topic, and rejecting some as unsuitable)
– negotiating meaning (finding out what people mean)
– supportive behaviour (acknowledging, helping)
– closing conversations.

In the following two settings, the first uses only present time and peripheral time. There is no personal time.

Setting 1

Present time	Two colleagues arrive in their office at work. The day is bright and clear, but there is a lot of snow on the ground.
Peripheral time	It snowed heavily during the night. There is a meeting in half an hour, at eight thirty.

Setting 2

Present time	Two strangers are sitting in a train on the way from Edinburgh to London. Another two people in the compartment are asleep. The train is stationary in the middle of nowhere. It is an early winter afternoon, and getting dark.

Peripheral time	The two strangers had seen each other, though not met, on the platform in Edinburgh. It was raining very hard, but has now stopped. The train has just braked very suddenly and come to a stop, though not at a station.
Personal time	A: You would like to talk to B. You are a visitor to Britain.
Personal time	B: You would be happy to talk to A and are thinking of what to say when the train stops. You live in Edinburgh and are travelling to London to visit relatives.

An example of a conversation based on setting 1 is given below. The topics raised are natural, and not a source of surprise. The speakers make allusion to the snow, and create images. The conversation is recognizably authentic, apart from the greeting and the obvious language mistakes. The first topic is about the snow and the difficulties it has created, but there are also other comments—'Very nice. The winter is beginning.' and 'It's beautiful when the sun is shining.' The change to the second topic, the meeting, is again quite natural and unforced, as is the speaker's indication that she wants to get away and prepare for the meeting.

Françoise	Good morning, Serge. How are you?
Serge	Good morning, fine. Fine. Hi, Françoise, how are you?
Françoise	Fine, thank you. Did you, er, do you see the snow in the streets?
Serge	Yes. Very nice. The winter is beginning.
Françoise	Yes, it . . . I had problems with, this morning, with my car.
Serge	With the car? Did you have gummi, snow gummi, winter gummi? [snow tyres]
Françoise	No. No, no. I had to go out . . . feet.
Serge	On feet.
Françoise	On foot. Yes.
Serge	Walking? You walked?
Françoise	Yes. Yes. And it was very, er, slippery.
Serge	Yes. I went with my car. It was very difficult to drive. It's nice. I liked it. I like it.
Françoise	It's beautiful when the sun is shining.
Serge	Yes.
Françoise	Did you prepare anything for this meeting?
Serge	No.

Françoise	Ah, yes. Because I have to prepare something, and as I arrived . . .
Serge	Too late . . .
Françoise	Too late.

Conclusion

In this chapter there has obviously only been limited space for what is a very rich area. Frameworks can be developed for a great variety of purposes, and are particularly helpful in devising relevant simulations for specific target groups—for example, product managers or production planners. It is important to remember that they are a tool, first to analyse what language the learner needs to be taught, then to organize the language, and finally to provide a framework for meaningful practice. They do not and cannot replace materials which are designed to input and explain structures and other language items. There will always be some learners who work better with them than others.

12 AUTHENTIC MATERIALS

Definition and use

Authentic material is any kind of material taken from the real world and not specifically created for the purpose of language teaching. It can be text, visuals, or audio material; it can be realia such as tickets, menus, maps, and timetables; or it can be objects such as products, equipment, components, or models. Some people say that as soon as a piece of authentic material has been altered in any way (for example, by cutting, selecting, simplifying, or transferring from one medium of communication to another), it immediately ceases to be authentic. However, any of these strategies may be applied if it can be justified in relation to the needs of learners.

For Business English training purposes, the authentic material that is most useful will be produced by companies for use by their employees, for client information, or for general publicity. However, material produced for public consumption but with a business content can also be drawn upon: for example, journals, newspapers, and off-air transmissions. A more detailed breakdown of types and sources of authentic material is given on pages 158–62.

There are several reasons why a trainer might use authentic material.

First, authentic texts (audio or written) will have a number of features that are often lacking in texts and dialogues created for learning English. They will exemplify the particular register to which they belong (academic, legal, or journalistic, etc.) and will often contain specific terminology and jargon and sometimes typical organizational features and sentence patterns. The language used will reflect the genuine purpose for which the material was created and will also target the expert reader or listener for whom it was intended. It will not be simplified or distorted by attempts to include structures or expressions aimed at the language learner. In short, authentic text will include the type of language which the learner may need to be exposed to, to develop skills for understanding, and possibly even to produce.

Second, the material may provide information about real-life situations or events. In this case, it is the content of the material rather than the language which is useful for the trainer or for the learner. The information conveyed is likely to be more accurate and to have high credibility, and will probably be more up-to-date than most Business English training materials. It may also be very relevant to the learner's special interests and can thus be used to fill gaps in materials published for learners of English.

Authentic material may provide the core of a very specialized course if the course objective is, for example, to develop skills for reading manuals, instructions, contracts, or financial reports, or to develop letter-writing or report-writing skills. At the other extreme, authentic material may be used only occasionally on a course—to supplement Business English material by adding interest and variety.

There are many more ways of using authentic materials other than as reading or listening comprehension exercises. For example, they can: provide a realistic context for a role-play, letter, or report; stimulate debate; provide information for a project or presentation; or practise the skills of describing, explaining, instructing, and exchanging information. (See pages 162–85 for more detail about ways of exploiting different kinds of authentic material.)

Types and sources

Below is a list of the different types and sources of authentic material that are appropriate for Business English teaching, together with suggestions for obtaining them.

Books

Business books may have been written for study purposes at colleges and universities, or may be aimed at people in work who want to brush up on their business knowledge or skills. Some may be very academic, some more practical, and some humorous. It may be possible to find them in a good general bookshop or (in the case of academic textbooks) in a university bookshop. Some can be found in libraries (for example, British Council, USIS, or university libraries). Clearly, the trainer would not want to use the whole book, but may find certain chapters, paragraphs, or diagrams in them that could be relevant to the learners. A list of such books is included in the Appendix.

The media

Newspapers, magazines, and specialist journals   Single items or articles, chosen for their relevance and interest, are most likely to be useful, but advertisements (for products or jobs), or illustrations and diagrams, may also be selected. English-language newspapers and magazines are available in major cities throughout the world, or can be ordered on subscription. Specialist journals are usually only available on subscription or from libraries.

Radio and TV   The BBC World Service has for many years provided an opportunity for listeners around the world to tune into authentic English. News broadcasts are particularly useful, but other kinds of information programmes can be exploited as well. Information about wavelengths and programmes can be obtained from local British Council offices and from the magazine *BBC Worldwide* (see Appendix).

With the advent of cable and satellite TV, it is now possible for viewers to tune into English-language news and documentary programmes in many countries. BBC World Service television is broadcast by satellite (and by cable in Europe), and aims to provide a worldwide service. Details of how to receive it, and information on programme schedules, can be obtained from the BBC at the address given in the Appendix under 'Further Viewing'. CBS news provides access to American English. (Note that there are laws restricting the recording of off-air programmes other than for personal use.)

Company-specific materials

This is a very broad category and covers many different types of materials.

The Annual Report   This contains company accounts, details of directors and company structure, changes made in the previous year, and a report on the financial standing of the company.

Product information   Most companies produce glossy brochures for their clients about their products and services. Some of these will have a general content aimed at non-specialists; others may contain specific technical information for people in the trade.

Newsletters and magazines or other PR material   We can distinguish between glossy magazines produced by companies for public consumption and more basic newsletters aimed at staff. Both contain news and general information about the company, its staff, and its products or services.

Company videos   Many large companies now produce videos for PR purposes, and these can provide useful classroom material. Some give general information about the company and its products, some describe the company's history, focus on its concerns for the environment, or show manufacturing processes. There will probably be an English-language version even if the company is registered in a non-English-speaking country. Some videos have no speech, only music as a background to the images portrayed.

All of the above material can be obtained direct from a company. They do not contain confidential material and can therefore be used without causing concern.

Correspondence   Letters may be routine, non-routine, formal, or informal, and can have a range of different functions. Faxes are not very different from letters, although they are usually shorter and less formal. Very few people use the telex machine nowadays.

Letters, faxes, etc. may be obtainable if the trainer has contacts within a company. Course participants who are at work can be asked to bring samples if relevant to the course.

Reports and memos   These may simply be short notes—not even expressed in sentences; routine reports may be written by completing a form; some reports are sent by electronic mail and are never committed to paper. On the other hand, a report may be a long and carefully considered document containing a lot of detailed information about, for example, finance, marketing, or technical developments. Some reports are for internal consumption only, while others are prepared for clients or for other companies co-operating in joint ventures, for example.

Both internal and external reports are likely to be confidential and the trainer will only get access to them if a learner has a specific need and brings them along to the course.

Minutes of Meetings   Sometimes these are composed in very formal language and make use of a number of conventions. In other situations, the minutes are brief and possibly even in note form. They usually report the topics discussed and the action taken. Depending on the nature of the meeting, they will probably be confidential.

Contracts   These may be standard or non-standard and can have varying degrees of complexity and obscurity. American contracts are the most lengthy and detailed, whilst the British ones may use more difficult legal jargon. Contracts produced in English by other legal systems are usually relatively easy to read.

It is easy to get hold of standard insurance, hiring and purchasing contracts, but specific contracts relating to financial transactions, buyer–supplier relations, joint venture relations, etc. are likely to have restricted access.

Manuals and written instructions   These are grouped together because they have a common purpose and similar use of instructional language, although they may refer to either technical or administrative procedures. Manuals are typically rather long and are commonly produced in print for a wide range of users. An example would be computer software manuals, produced by the software house for its users worldwide. Instructions for using and maintaining equipment or machines could also be included in this category. Other kinds of instructions, however, are more temporary and usually shorter. They may be issued by the parent company to its subsidiaries, detailing procedures for carrying out routine tasks—for example, accounting and book-keeping. They may be issued in the form of an internal memo.

It is not difficult to get access to manuals if learners need to work with them: usually they can be provided by the learners, the company or training institution, or by the supplier. Company instructions for internal use are more likely to be confidential, but it should be possible to obtain examples if an employee has a special need.

Public information material

This category comprises all types of documents, brochures, leaflets, and video materials which are supplied by governments or national institutions for the general public. It is clearly a very wide-ranging category, but examples which are relevant for Business English are as follows:

– Tourist information (lists of restaurants and hotels, maps, information

about tourist sights, history and geography of a region, tourist videos, timetables, etc.)
– Information produced about the London Stock Exchange and Lloyds of London (educational videos can also be purchased—see Appendix)
– Information about postal and telecommunications services
– Information produced by banks about accounts, loans, financial services, etc.
– Customs and VAT forms and regulations
– Information produced by electricity companies and water boards (for example, about environment, energy saving)

These can be useful sources of material for people who work in the United Kingdom or sometimes travel to the United Kingdom or other English-speaking countries. Some kinds of information may be available in English in other countries—especially tourist information.

Recording live events on audio or video

Depending on the training situation, it may be possible to gain access to live events and situations which would provide useful material in the classroom. Examples are: lectures, seminars, and demonstrations (useful in the case of students and trainees); company visits—especially to a workshop or factory; and (if not too confidential) meetings and presentations. If the trainer has access to a camcorder, video camera, or even just an audio tape recorder, these events can be exploited as often as desired. The results may require a certain amount of editing (particularly for audio recordings, which are more difficult to use successfully without the visual element), but can provide excellent examples of authentic spoken language. Commentaries on professionally-made videos or TV broadcasts are scripted and therefore represent a different variety of English.

Selection and exploitation of authentic materials

When selecting material to use, it is very important to keep in mind the three key questions:

1 Who is it for?
2 What is the training purpose?
3 How can the material be exploited?

Ways of exploiting material will depend on the type and content of the material, and a successful exploitation will have to relate to the needs of the learners in terms of skills requirements, language requirements, level, and interests.

Text materials

Text materials provide a model of authentic written language. The use of text materials and their exploitation, therefore, needs to be seen in relation to the needs of the learners. Do the learners need to develop reading skills? If the answer is 'yes', then the text can be presented in its original form (or edited for low-level learners), together with suitable reading tasks or activities.

Depending on its content, the text could be used for language activities which focus on the vocabulary, structures, or functions it contains. The trainer would need to think about what is most useful for the learners and whether they need to use this language actively or merely be able to recognize its meaning when reading. Language which is only found in written texts should not be the focus of an oral production activity.

However, a large proportion of Business English learners need speaking and listening skills, and to provide this kind of practice, the text will have to be exploited or adapted in some other way. For example:

1 The text could be used by the trainer only for its information content (i.e. it is not seen by the learners).

2 If the learners need listening skills rather than reading skills, then the teacher could use the content of the text to present information orally to the learners. (Note that if the text is read aloud and recorded word for word on tape, it does not provide a model of oral language, so it will be necessary to phrase the ideas in different words.)

3 Facts, figures, or situations from the text could be used to devise role plays. (See the example at the end of this chapter.)

4 If there are diagrams or charts accompanying the text, information-transfer activities could be devised. An example of an information-transfer exercise is one where the learners are given a chart which has some information missing and they complete it with facts or figures from the text.

5 Information-transfer activities can be based on an oral version of the text, given by the trainer or another learner (i.e. as a listening task).

Both (4) and (5) could be followed up by asking the learners to present the information in the completed charts in their own words. The trainer can help or support with details from the text. Learners could complete different charts and then describe them to each other.

6 Jigsaw reading: the text is divided into parts and different parts handed out to different learners to read and take notes. The learners then use their notes to pass on the information orally to each other and to work

together to build up a summary of the complete text or to answer questions on the complete text.

7 Texts (particularly news items and magazine articles) can be used to stimulate discussion and debate, and to practise summarizing and forecasting possible outcomes, and making comparisons with their own experiences.

8 Reading and oral practice can be followed up by a writing task (if appropriate): preparing a written summary; writing a letter to the newspaper or magazine; writing a report for the company; or (if the text is itself a letter or report) replying to it or commenting on it.

Different types of text material are evaluated below in terms of which groups of learners could most benefit from using them, what teaching purposes (in terms of target language and skills) they could be used for, and what kinds of activities can be developed to achieve the teaching purposes.

1 Books, articles from journals, newspapers, etc.

These are particularly useful for pre-experience learners if the content is relevant. They are also useful for job-experienced learners, especially at managerial level, but should be selected according to needs. A prerequisite to setting a reading task based on a book extract or magazine article should be that the learner would be interested in reading the text if it were in his or her own language.

Table 12.1: Language activities using books and articles

Skills	Language	Activities
Reading: skim/scan, gist reading, detailed reading	Vocabulary	Jigsaw reading Information transfer Role play
Summarizing Information exchange Discussion Writing reports, summaries, memos	Comparison Forecasting Fact v. opinion Verb tenses Modal verbs Conjunctions Reference markers	

2 Pictures, charts, diagrams, etc.

These are useful for producing language, not for providing a model (unless accompanied by a text). They will appeal especially to learners who are visualizers, or who work a lot with visual material—for example, engineers and technical people, systems designers, sales and marketing staff. Charts containing figures will be appropriate for finance staff and others who have to present financial or sales results. Visual materials are also important for pre-experience learners who will later enter these fields.

Table 12.2: Language activities using visual materials

Skills	Language	Activities
Presenting information	Numbers	Information transfer
Information exchange	Describing trends	Pair/groupwork
Writing reports	Comparing	Presenting with
Listening	Contrasting	overhead projector
	Describing cause–effect	

3 Advertisements

Job advertisements can be used with pre-experience learners who may want to apply for jobs in English. They can stimulate letter writing, preparation of a CV in English, and even interview role plays.

Product advertisements can be used for making comparisons, discussing advertising techniques, or relating to the learners' own products. They are thus useful with a wide range of learners, both pre-experience and job-experienced.

Table 12.3: Language activities using advertisements

Skills	Language	Activities
Reading	Vocabulary	Pair/groupwork
Information exchange	Numbers	Product presentations
Discussion	Comparing	Role play
Interviewing	Contrasting	Creating own
Letter-writing	Evaluating	advertisements
	Describing features	Writing CVs and letters

4 Realia

Realia such as airline tickets, hotel information, timetables, and menus are useful for anyone who needs English to travel abroad, particularly if their language level is pre-intermediate or below. They are very useful for secretaries and others who may need to make travel arrangements. Menus are useful for business people who have to entertain clients in restaurants. Menus in the learners' mother tongue can also be used to practise explaining food, etc. to English-speaking visitors.

Table 12.4: Language activities using realia

Skills	Language	Activities
Telephoning	Times, dates	Role play:
Writing letters, faxes	Requesting	making/changing
Discussing schedules	Clarifying	bookings, asking for
Social survival	Confirming	information, ordering
	Suggesting	food in a restaurant
	Explaining	

5 Company material

This is most likely to be available and appropriate to trainers working with job-experienced learners in-company. Some examples may be interesting for pre-experience learners preparing for future jobs.

Annual reports   These are especially useful for finance and accounting staff, for people whose job involves assessing companies from an investment point of view (several reports would be needed for comparison), and for any employees who need to be able to present his or her own company.

Table 12.5: Language activities using annual reports

Skills	Language	Activities
Information exchange	Numbers	Pair/groupwork
Talking about accounts	Accounting/Finance	Presenting
Understanding financial	vocabulary	accounts/graphs/diagrams
reports	Describing trends	Information transfer
Making presentations	Company structure	Completing text
	Tenses: past and	Comparing accounting
	present perfect	systems
	Forecasting	

Contracts   These are useful for company lawyers and pre-experience learners studying company law. They are also useful for buyers, suppliers, and others who may need to refer to contracts in their work.

Table 12.6: Language activities using contracts

Skills	Language	Activities
Reading contracts:	Specific terminology	Search for answers to
scanning, detailed	for: terms, conditions,	specific questions
reading	obligation, inclusions,	Explain/summarize
Negotiating	restrictions, reference.	terms, provisions
Writing letters	Conditional sentences	Role play: negotiating
	Modal verbs	changes to a contract
	Clarifying	
	Suggesting	

Correspondence   Correspondence is particularly useful for secretaries and commercial staff—pre-experience or job-experienced. It is also useful for anyone else who has to deal with their own correspondence (fairly common even for managers now).

Table 12.7: Language activities using correspondence

Skills	Language	Activities
Reading letters	Letter conventions	Jigsaw reading
Writing letters	Style	Information transfer
Telephoning	Organizational features	Completing a letter
Exchanging information		Role play
		Replying to a letter

Reports and memos   These are only relevant to people who have to read them or write them. Check what kind of reports the learners have to deal with, and obtain samples. Pre-experience learners may have to write reports for their courses of study, but these may have a very different style and structure from company reports.

Table 12.8: Language activities using reports and memos

Skills	Language	Activities
Reading for information	(depends on type and content)	Jigsaw reading
Report writing	Organizational features	Restructuring a report
Telephoning	Style	Rewriting
Discussion skills	Vocabulary	Comparing oral/written language
Presenting		Role play: meeting/telephone call to discuss report

Minutes of meetings   These will be important for those who have to read them (people who attend international meetings) and for those who have to write them (mainly secretaries, but also managers, technical staff, etc.).

Table 12.9: Language activities using minutes

Skills	Language	Activities
Listening	Reported speech	Acting out the minuted meeting
Summarizing	Passives	Taking minutes from a video or role play
Writing minutes	Past tenses	

Manuals and instructions   These are only useful for those who have to read or write them. Check what the learners have to deal with and obtain samples. Written instructions could be reproduced as oral instructions if this is appropriate to the learners' needs.

Table 12.10: Language activities using instructions

Skills	Language	Activities
Following instructions (oral/written) Giving instructions Explaining Demonstrating	Imperatives Modal verbs Modal passive Prepositions Time clauses Conditionals Sequence markers Specific vocabulary	Search for answers to questions Information transfer: complete flow charts/create flow charts Ordering in correct sequence Matching written/aural/visual

Product brochures and specifications   The trainer can make use of the text, the specifications (figures and technical details), or pictures and diagrams relating to a company's products. These materials are more obviously relevant to job-experienced learners, but could provide a stimulus for pre-experience learners too.

Table 12.11: Language activities using brochures

Skills	Language	Activities
Reading for information Describing/explaining Presenting information Negotiating Telephoning	Numbers Vocabulary for size, appearance, function, features Comparing/contrasting Stating advantages Describing how it works	Search for answers to questions Information transfer Pair/groupwork Matching text to visual Sales presentations Role play: sales negotiation, product development meeting, ordering by telephone, answering product enquiries

PR materials   Some of these can be of general interest to both company employees and people outside the company. Brochures about the company's environment policy, for example, could be interesting to some pre-experience learners.

For examples of language activities, see Table 12.1 on newspapers, magazines, and journals, page 164.

Audio and video materials

Authentic audio and video materials provide a model of spoken language,
which differs in many features from written language. However, as already
pointed out, scripted audio or video tapes do not represent natural speech,
and may even have more in common with written language: sentences
will be complete, there will be no rephrasing or repetition, no hesitations
or false starts, and no grammatical mistakes. In media recordings, natural
speech is likely to be heard in interview situations, but apart from this,
nearly everything will have been scripted. There is even a recognizable
style for TV reportage, which may or may not be an appropriate model
for business people. Recordings made at live events are much more likely
to reflect all the imperfections of natural speech. However, professionally-
recorded material provides useful listening practice and can be a stimulus
for many oral and written activities.

It should be noted that the language used in authentic audios and videos
recorded for a native-speaker audience will generally be too fast and too
complex for low-level learners to follow. If it is appropriate, low-level
learners could be exposed to such videos, but with a relatively simple task
(for example, gist listening), and very short extracts should be chosen. For
learners at any level, a short extract (three to five minutes of audio or
video material) per session will be sufficient. To sit through half an hour
of video demands too much concentration. An exception can be made for
high-level learners who need to practise note-taking or minute-taking
skills.

As with text materials, audio and video recordings can be used simply as
background information for the trainer, or for listening practice, for language work, or as a stimulus for a variety of oral activities. Video recordings can be played with or without sound: without sound gives the
viewers the opportunity to guess what is going on from the actions and
body language of the people in the film, and to guess their relationships
and their reactions to new events. This can be especially useful in the context of social English and for developing cross-cultural awareness. Videos
of a manufacturing process can be played without sound for learners to
create their own commentary, or simply to point and name if they are at a
low level. Both audio and video recordings can be stopped at strategic
points to ask learners to predict what will happen next, or what will be
said next (for example, after a question is asked). The freeze frame facility

on a video recorder is useful for discussing a particular scene, pointing and naming things, or talking about the people in the film and what they are doing.

As with text material, the subject-matter of a video can be exploited in a number of ways. Information-transfer activities can be devised; role plays can be set up; learners can be asked to summarize, to write reports, to act out scenes using their own words, and so on.

Some specific ideas are given in the tables below.

1 TV and radio news

Clearly, this is best when 'fresh' and would normally be recorded on the same day that it will be used in class. It is especially useful for journalists, PR staff, the information services staff of companies, economists, and others who have to follow reports or make reports themselves. In general interest terms, it can be useful for almost anybody since people who travel need to be able to follow and talk about current events. Businesspeople often complain that they find it hard to carry on a conversation during a business lunch, for example: news items can often provide useful topics for conversation. The implications of news items for business, for companies, or for a nation provide useful discussion points.

Table 12.12: Language activities using TV and radio news

Skills	Language	Activities
Listening for gist	Vocabulary: political,	Pair/groupwork
Detailed listening	economic, geographic,	Information transfer
Summarizing	etc.	Comparison of different
Reporting	Tenses: past,	reports
Discussion skills	present perfect	Preparing own report
Conversation skills	Forecasting	(oral/written)
	Fact v. opinion	
	Cause and effect	

2 Documentaries

These will be selected according to the relevance of their information content. The trainer might want to focus on a business or economic theme, or on something of wider interest (for example, the EC, the environment). The learners could have a special interest—for example in a foreign country that they do business with, or will travel to. Documentaries about new scientific or technical developments are useful for people working in a related technical field.

Table 12.13: Language activities using documentaries

Skills	Language	Activities
Listening for information	Specific vocabulary	Search for answers to
Describing	Tenses: past,	specific questions
Explaining	present perfect	Taking notes
Summarizing	Forecasting	Information transfer
Interviewing	Comparing	Completing chart of
Discussion skills	Cause and effect	arguments for/against
Writing reports	Questioning	Describing with sound
	Giving opinions	down
		Role play: interviews,
		meetings, debates

3 Company videos

These are mainly useful for people working in the company which has produced the video, or in its subsidiaries or affiliates. They could be useful for customers of the company. Some company videos provide investment information, and this could be of interest to learners working in the fields of finance or banking.

The table given for documentaries (12.13) applies also to company videos.

4 Public information videos

These are produced by, for example, the London Stock Exchange, The British Department of Trade and Industry, and the Tourist Boards of some regions.

The Square Mile is an educational pack consisting of a video and booklets with further information and questions about the City of London, the Stock Exchange, and Lloyds of London. This kind of material is particularly useful for pre-experience students on Business Studies courses who have a reasonably good level of English. It will probably have less appeal to job-experienced learners unless they are working in or deal with this area.

The British Department of Trade and Industry has produced some videos about the European Community, mainly directed at British companies who need to be more informed about changes in trading practice. This kind of material could be useful in countries thinking of entering the EC, for use either with pre-experience or job-experienced learners.

Tourist videos will have a more general application, and could be used to stimulate practice in talking about their own country to foreign visitors. In this respect, videos of the mother country are more valuable than videos of Britain.

For a more detailed breakdown of possible skills, language, and activities, see Table 12.13 on Documentaries.

Examples of tasks and activities

The last section of this chapter will give some examples of tasks and activities developed to exploit authentic materials.

1 *Using authentic material to develop speaking skills*

Basing a telephone role play on an authentic fax

FACSIMILE COMMUNICATION
JAPANESE MOTORS LIMITED, TOKYO, JAPAN

TO: MR. B. HENRIKSEN   DATE: MAY 18\   PAGE 1 OF 1
      JAPANESE MOTORS   OUR REF: ISZ·6533–
      DISTRIBUTING AGENT,   FROM: SAKURI\KATSU
      NORWAY
COPY TO:

                                    FAX. NO: 47 2 8964728

SUBJECT: YR SEAT TRIM ORDERS

THANK YOU FOR YR ORDERS, 3 ROLLS OF SEAT
CLOTH TRIM.

WE HAVE PLACED THE ABOVES ORDERS ON THE
FOLLOWING SCHEDULES.

O\NO	Q'TY	SHIP BY	AROUND
2b035	1 ROLL	AIR	JUL 2
2b03b	2 ROLLS	SEA	JUL 15

PLS REFER TO OUR FAX ISZ–4218–8b OF NOV 28\
IT'S NECESSARY 2 MONTHS LEAD TIME USUALLY, HOWEVER,
CONSIDERING YR SITUATION, WE PUT YR ORDERS VERY URGENTLY,
AS POSSIBLE AS WE CAN.
YR KIND UNDERSTANDING WOULD BE APPRECIATED.
REGARDS.

Activity

Objective	To practise negotiating on the telephone.
Level	Lower intermediate to upper intermediate.
Target audience	Job-experienced learners who will need to make purchase orders by telephone. Pre-experience learners preparing for this kind of work.
When	After introducing basic telephone language and practising simple telephone activities (e.g. message-taking, making enquiries, and exchanging information); when you want to extend the learners' ability to deal with more complex matters on the telephone.
Time	45 minutes.
Preparation	Discuss with the learners what happens when an agent or distributor receives goods that are not perfect.
	Give the fax to the learners to read. Deal with any vocabulary ('seat', 'trim', 'roll', 'lead time', etc.). Discuss the situation referred to by the fax. What do the learners think happened before this fax was sent? Why is the Japanese company sending rolls of cloth? What was the problem? Could there be any other solution? Why does Mr Henriksen need the cloth urgently?
Procedure	Explain to the learners that they are going to role play a telephone call. Divide the group into pairs and tell the pairs that one will play the part of Mr Henriksen, and the other the part of Mr Sakurai. They will imagine the conversation that might have preceded this fax.
	Hand out the role cards and allow about five minutes for preparation. The role-play can be done by pairs working simultaneously: (1) in the classroom, back to back; or (2) using the internal telephone system; or (3) in a language laboratory.
	On a one-to-one course, the trainer should play one of the roles. It is useful to record the conversations for feedback and review.

2 *Using authentic material to practise extracting information from a text*

Understanding computer manuals

```
With the Mail Function you can:
Electronically send letters and documents to an individual
or group. You can specify a priority of relative importance
(high, low, and so on); a class (first class, registered, or
certified); security (private or none); and you can encrypt
mail. By using the directory, you can locate users and
create a mailing list.

Terminology

• Mailbox — A file which is created by the system in the
  folder your.dsk. An incoming.mbx (mailbox) file is created
  when you receive mail. An outgoing.mbx file is created
  when you file a copy of the mail you send. A phone.mbx file
  is created when you receive a phone message. A
  phonelog.mbx is created when you file a copy of the phone
  message you send.
• Encryption — Coding which requires the recipient to use a
  keyword for decoding so they can open the mail. Further
  explanation is given in R5-5 (3 of 3), ''Fields of the
  Electronic Mail Screen''.
```

Activity

Objective	To practise extracting information from a computer manual text.
Level	Elementary to intermediate.
Target audience	Job-experienced people working with computers (for example, in finance or clerical jobs). Pre-experience learners studying how to use computers or word processors.
When	The learners will have already acquired a reasonable vocabulary of the terms found in the relevant computer manuals, and will have done previous reading activities based on understanding key structures and functions.
Time	20–30 minutes.
Procedure	Hand out the task sheet and text. Point out that learners need not read the whole text first. They should read the items on the task sheet and look for the answer in the relevant section of the text. (See sample instructions below.)

Sample instructions for task

Which of these things can you do with the Mail Function? Look for the answers in the text on the next page.

Write down the number of the line where the information can be found.

		line number
1	Send a letter electronically to a single person	1
2	Send the same letter electronically to several people	_____
3	Receive telephone messages	_____
4	Access other people's letters and messages	_____
5	Send confidential mail that only one person can read	_____
6	Find out who are the other people who have access to the system	_____
7	Collect the names of people that you often want to send letters to	_____
8	Show how important your letter is	_____
9	Send pictures and graphics	_____
10	Store copies of all the messages you receive	_____

Photocopiable material   © Oxford University Press 1994

3 Using authentic material to develop listening skills

Using graphs or charts

Activity

Objective	To introduce or practise recognition of the language of economic trends (increase/decrease; vocabulary such as 'to reach a peak'; correct use of prepositions 'to', 'by', 'in', etc.).
Level	Lower intermediate to intermediate.
Target audience	Job-experienced learners working in economic or financial areas. Pre-experience learners studying economics or business studies.

Jan. 1992   Jan. 1993

Jan. 1993   Jan. 94

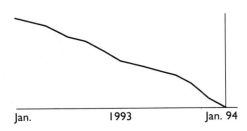

Jan.   1993   Jan. 94

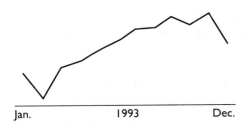

Jan.   1993   Dec.

Photocopiable material

When	After presenting the language of trends and before asking the learners to try to produce the language themselves.
Time	Listening only: 20 minutes. With stage 3: 45 minutes.
Source material/ adaptation	Graphs showing economic trends taken from newspapers and finance journals (e.g. *The Economist*). The titles of the graphs have been removed, and also some details such as numerical values given on the Y axis. A script describing the graphs has to be prepared and may be recorded on tape. (See sample script below.)
Preparation	Start a brief discussion on the economy and ask what factors are often used as economic indicators (elicit 'inflation', 'unemployment', etc.). Explain as necessary: retail sales, industrial output, unemployment, average earnings.
Procedure	Give the graphs to the learners. Read or play a recording of the script. Learners follow and identify what each

graph refers to. In a second stage, learners can add numerical values to the graphs. As a third stage, they may be asked to describe the graphs themselves.

Sample script

As you can see, unemployment has declined steadily since January 1993. At that time it stood at 9 per cent; a year later, in January 1994, it had reached a very satisfactory 7 per cent.

Unfortunately the figures for industrial output during the same period are not so good. After hitting a low at the end of January 1993, the industrial output index increased to 108.5 points a month later, and rose steadily to almost 111 points in the middle of the year. The index fluctuated during the next three or four months, then fell dramatically, bringing the figure back to 109.8 points at the end of the year.

Over the period in question, retail sales have shown a general upwards trend, but with seasonal fluctuations. Retail sales reached a peak of 141 points at the end of September 1993, fell slightly in October, rose again in November, and, surprisingly, fell dramatically in December. However, they rose again to 140 points in the first month of 1994.

The increase in average earnings has also shown a movement upwards. At the start of January 1992 the increase over the previous year was 7.5 per cent. This rose slightly at the end of March, then remained constant for six months, rising again to 8.5 per cent in the last three months of 1992. This remained constant for five months, and, despite rising to 9.25 per cent in August and September, finished the year at 8.75 per cent.

Sample instructions for tasks

The graphs show four aspects of the British economy:

– retail sales
– industrial output index
– unemployment
– average earnings (percentage increase over previous year)

1 Listen to your trainer's presentation, and label the graphs.

2 Listen again and fill in any numbers you hear on the vertical axis of each graph.

4 *Using authentic materials to improve learners' comprehension of presentations*

Adapting an article for oral presentation

Activity

Objective	To practise listening to a longer text and extracting specific information. To extend vocabulary relating to logistics and distribution.
Level	Intermediate to upper intermediate.
Target audience	Job-experienced people or pre-experience learners who need to be able to follow lectures and presentations and who may be interested in logistics and distribution.
Time	Listening only: 15 minutes. With other follow-up: one hour.
Source material/ adaptation	An article from a business journal. The article itself is not given to the learner. The trainer uses the information in the article to prepare a script for a presentation (adapting the language so that it is more appropriate to an oral presentation) and this can be recorded on tape. The diagram is copied from the article and its labels are erased (see below).
Procedure	1) Learners listen to the tape and label the diagram. 2) Learners answer comprehension questions and questions that focus on language features (e.g. vocabulary) used in the tape. (Not included here.) 3) Learners use the diagram to practise making their own mini-presentations.

DISTRIBUTION

How a streamlined logistics system can make all the difference

Sub-contracting was the secret for newly merged French and German interests in the field of consumer electronics

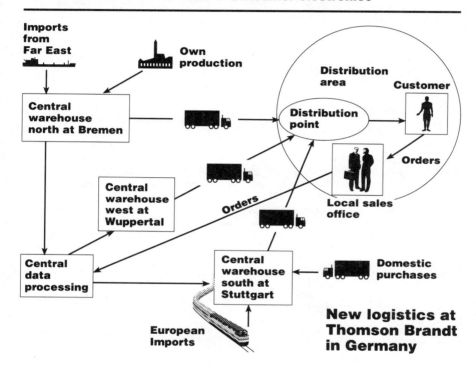

In the great drive to contain costs, managers always get around, in the end, to looking at inventory, handling and distribution figures. These can be horrendous and, in the case of some marketing-oriented companies, can constitute the bulk of fixed overheads.

The problem is worsened in Europe by the existence of the national boundaries of 16 sovereign states and, more recently, by the wave of takeovers, mergers and the struggle for market share that has afflicted many industries, foremost among them consumer electronics.

Now one company – Saba, a German sales subsidiary of the Paris-based consumer electronics giant Thomson Brandt – has come to grips with its own distribution problems and, in the process, established a pattern for two other Thomson brands, Nordmende and Telefunken, to follow. A

fourth brand, Dual, will be integrated into the system next year.

All four brands were acquired by Thomson Brandt in the past six years, as part of its drive into consumer electronics. Nordmende was purchased in 1978. Saba was acquired from General Telephone & Electronics Co. (GTE) of the United States in 1981. Dual – which, like Nordmende, was independently owned – joined the fold in 1982. And Telefunken was acquired from the ailing electronics giant, AEG, only last year.

By subcontracting and streamlining its entire distribution effort, Saba is claiming to have saved substantial costs and improved customer service. The streamlining spanned nearly three years from initial studies to proof of savings.

With Thomson Brandt's results now proven, other manufacturers in Germany and elsewhere are showing keener interest in rationalizing distribution systems, says Horst Gade, a senior consultant at Knight Wendling (formerly Knight Weggenstein), which worked with Saba in the restructuring. Knight Wendling is now deeply involved with a German chocolate maker to devise a similar streamlining. And Thomson Brandt, impressed by Saba's improvements, is considering a revamp of its distribution systems throughout Europe.

Knight Wendling has high hopes of persuading companies in other European countries to do more to improve effectiveness, and cut costs, on the distribution front. "Even small companies, employing fewer than 200 people, can make significant savings if they look at the problem as a whole," says Detlef Munchow, director of Knight Wendling's London office. He says stock levels in Britain, for example, could be reduced by as much as 30%, simply by turning over stock much faster (see box).

Essentially, what Saba has done is route its television sets, videos, hi-fi equipment and radios through just three central warehouses, then ship them overnight to regional distribution centres, for onward delivery to customers by local transport the following day. "We have achieved savings of 20% so far," says Dieter Loeding, Saba's logistic manager. That means a reduction of millions of marks in warehousing, materials handling and distribution. Saba will not cite precise savings.

Why materials handling costs money

Detlef Munchow, of Knight Wendling's London office, produces the following figures to illustrate what he sees as room for improvement in materials handling and distribution among British companies, for example:

Stock turnover ratio in engineering companies

Britain	3–6 times a year
West Germany	10–12 times a year
Japan	15–20 times a year

Total cost of materials handling and distribution in British manufacturing companies

Up to 20% of turnover
Up to 30% of value added

Other statistics
Seventy to 80% of the material lead time in manufacturing is time of waiting. By bringing material into flow more quickly, it would be possible to decrease stock levels in British industry by 20% to 30%, Munchow claims.

So successful has the company been in this endeavour that some of Thomson Brandt's rivals in consumer electronics, including Philips, ITT and Grundig, have been taking note of the reorganization. "We get a lot of inquiries from them," says Loeding. "They are very interested in adopting some of our ideas."

A few years ago, indeed, Grundig was touting the idea of a distribution system for the whole of Europe that would embrace every company that wanted to participate. But this came to nothing. So Thomson Brandt, whose products account for about 25% of the German market in consumer electronics, decided to make its own improvements. Saba, with $172 million annual sales in Germany and $276 million sales worldwide last year, emerged as the pathfinder under a new chief executive, Dr. Alexander Lentze, who arrived three years ago.

Thorough analysis

"Setting in train a thorough analysis of the distribution costs was the first thing I did," Lentze remarks. He points out that Saba is a sales company, the manufacturing being done by another Thomson Brandt affiliate, Dagfu. As such, its major fixed costs *are* those concerned with logistics. So Lentze was coming to grips with the main costs base.

Saba had been relying on a central warehouse, comprising 23,000 cubic metres, and 17 smaller regional warehouses, totalling 16,000 cubic metres of capacity. Products were transported by a forwarding agent from the central warehouse to the regional warehouses, where a fleet of 19 company trucks distributed 86,000 cubic metres of equipment, in 80,000 separate consignments, to 3,000 outlets, most of them retail stores.

Although this system worked smoothly, the cost of maintaining the warehouse space, the trucking fleet and the attendant staff was burdensome. Loeding points out that about half of Saba's business is done in just four months of the year. For the other eight months, expensive fixed assets were standing idle or underutilized. In addition, there were shortcomings in customer service. Deliveries could be made only two or three times a week, resulting in delays of several days if an order missed one delivery.

Knight Wendling's Gade, along with two other consultants and a good internal team from Thomson Brandt, spent six months, off and on, analysing the old distribution system and working out the new concept. Then a further 18 months were spent on implementation. "As well as working closely with the Saba people, there were many coordination meetings with the other brands, to ensure we weren't crossing too many wires," Gade says.

As a result of these deliberations, Saba closed all its regional warehouses and comcentrated inventory at three locations – a warehouse near Stuttgart that handles imports from Italy and Germany; Bremen, in north Germany, where the warehouse is near a manufacturing plant and its proximity to the port enables it to handle imports from the Far East; and Wuppertal, which exists to serve the many customers in the western part of the Federal Republic.

All the brands currently involved in the scheme now send their products from the factory to these warehouses, with the exception that Telefunken still runs its own warehouse at Hannover, storing products from its factory at Celle, rather than use the Bremen warehouse.

Using outsiders

From these warehouses the branded products are trucked by night to 24 distribution points, all over western Germany, then transferred into smaller vehicles for onward transmission to customers within a 50 to 80 kilometre radius. And apart from the on-line network that transmits orders via a central computer, Saba staff are not involved in this operation, which is handled by two forwarding companies, Dietrich in southern Germany and Kuehne Nagel in the north.

"There was no problem persuading the company to use outsiders because the basic philosophy of Thomson Brandt is that they are specialists in electronic equipment," Gade says. "and not distribution experts. So they said from the beginning that if experienced partners could be found to distribute their products in an economical way, that was okay by them."

There was a problem, however, in persuading Saba's own branch officers that the change would be a good one. The marketing people objected that putting several brands on one truck was just not acceptable.

"Their argument was that customers were used to our own trucks delivering the goods, and that we might even lose sales to other brands," Lentze says. "But I saw this as emotional, rather than practical, resistance from our people."

To get beneath the unthinking emotion, he called two-day seminars that were attended by the branch officers, and invited them to spell out all their reservations, which were then dissected and examined. "The object of the exercise was to reinforce the advantages of change and minimize any disadvantages," Lentze says. "Maybe there is a genuine disadvantage insofar as the relationship between the salesman/rep and the merchandiser at head office is interrupted, to some extent. The man in the field liked to say to the customer, 'Okay, I will get on the phone to head office and speed things up'. But, because everything was speeded up, that was no longer necessary. I can understand why some people felt that, in a sense, their job was being devalued."

Since the new logistics system was introduced, however, the level of complaints and minor delivery emergencies has fallen, says Lentze. As for the argument that customers would turn to other brands, nobody at Saba believes that any more. Now, the company is able to offer a 48-hour delivery service. From Wuppertal, indeed, it is a 24-hour service. This has led to far more satisfied customers than disgruntled ones.

Sample tapescript

JW   Good morning. Can I start by introducing myself? My name's John Webber, and I'm a consultant at Knight Wendling, which, as you know, is a business systems consultancy firm. My firm has recently completed a project in which we worked together with the German company, Saba. Saba, you may know, is a German Sales subsidiary of Thomson-Brandt, which specializes in consumer electronic goods—TVs, Hifi systems, that sort of thing.

So, what I'd like to do today is to describe briefly the project we undertook with Saba which was to streamline the distribution system.

Well, first let me explain the distribution system which Saba used to have and why we thought it necessary to change the system.

In the past, Saba had one central warehouse comprising 23,000 cubic metres, and 17 smaller warehouses totalling 16,000 cubic metres of capacity.

Products were transported from the central warehouse to the regional warehouses by a forwarding agent. From the regional warehouses, a fleet of 19 company trucks were used to distribute the equipment—altogether about 86,000 cubic metres of equipment would be delivered each year, in 80,000 separate consignments to 3,000 different destinations—mostly small retail outlets.

DJ Sorry to interrupt, but could you give us those figures again, please?

JW Certainly. That was 86,000 cubic metres of equipment in 80,000 separate consignments going to 3,000 outlets.

DJ And how many trucks did you say?

JW 19 trucks, owned by the company.

Well, this system worked smoothly enough, but it was expensive. The warehouse space had to be maintained, and the trucks. The staff had to be paid, of course, on a year-round basis.

Now, one of the features of the consumer electronics industry is that about half the year's trading is done during four months of the year—the four months leading up to Christmas. During the rest of the year, the other 8 months, company capital was tied up in warehousing and trucks—expensive fixed assets—which were not being used to full capacity. In addition to these problems, there were often delays in delivery. Deliveries were made two or three times a week, so if an order missed one delivery, this could result in a delay of several days. So customer dissatisfaction was another problem.

Now, Saba—as I've said before—is a sales company. And as a sales company, the major fixed costs are those concerned with logistics. And that's where cost savings had to be made.

So what changes did we make?

As you can see from the diagram, Saba has now closed all its regional warehouses, and its inventory is concentrated at three locations.

There's one warehouse near Stuttgart that handles imports from Italy, and domestic purchases from within Germany; one warehouse at Bremen, in the north—that's near the manufacturing plant and also near the port so it can handle imports from the Far East; then, there's a third warehouse at Wuppertal which serves customers in the western part of Germany . . .

DJ I have a question . . .

JW Yes?

DJ Saba is one of several Thomson-Brandt subsidiaries, isn't that right?

JW Yes.

DJ Could you tell us whether the other Thomson-Brandt subsidiaries, like Telefunken, have also been involved in this project?

JW Yes, they have. Saba was the first one to rationalize its distribution system. But Telefunken, and another subsidiary, Nordmende, have now been integrated into the new system too; and a fourth subsidiary—Dual—will be integrated next year. All the brands involved in the scheme now send their products from the factory to one of these three warehouses.

DJ And who does the distribution? A forwarding agent?

JW Two forwarding companies, actually—one in the north and one in the south. The products are carried on big trucks from the warehouses to 24 distribution points. Then, at each distribution point, the goods are transferred on to smaller vehicles and distributed to the customers, who are all within a radius of 50 to 80 kilometres.

DJ And the whole system is controlled by computer?

JW That's right. There's an on-line network which transmits orders to a central computer.

DJ And would you mind telling us what improvements there were—as a result of the changes?

JW As far as costs are concerned, we've achieved savings of 20 per cent so far. In addition, we can offer a 48-hour delivery service—in some areas it's only 24 hours—and we've got a lot more satisfied customers.

DJ Hmm. That's pretty impressive . . . [FADE]

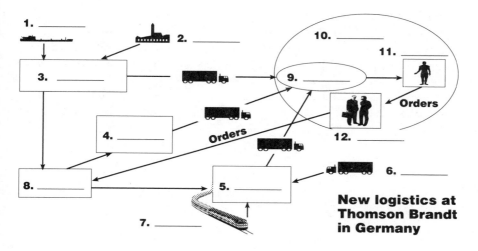

New logistics at
Thomson Brandt
in Germany

5 Using authentic material to extend letter-writing vocabulary

Completing a business letter

Activity

Objective	To extend knowledge of letter-writing vocabulary; to develop awareness of the differences between spoken and written language.
Level	Intermediate.
Target audience	Anyone who has to write business letters.
Time	30 minutes.
Adaptation of source	Some words have been omitted to create a gap-filling task. If you are going to create this kind of task yourself, it will be important to choose a suitable letter (in terms of content and language difficulty) and to select words to be omitted according to: (a) which words can be guessed from the context, and (b) which words the learners need to have in their active vocabulary.
Procedure	Learners can work in pairs to try to guess the missing words. They should be allowed to use a dictionary. To make the task easier for lower-level learners, or to focus more on developing passive vocabulary, a list of the missing words can be supplied. The task will then be to recognize and select the best word to fill each gap.

Sample instructions for task

Read the letter from the London branch of a bank. Try to find suitable words or phrases to complete the letter. If you cannot find any suitable words, your trainer will give you a list to choose from.

[*name and address of company.*]

Attention: Mrs [*name of recipient*]

Dear [*name*]
Re: <u>**RETAIL BANKING**</u>

On the attached you will find the Bank's proposed Schedule of Charges which will
as from 1st January 1994, and will be   annually.

We very much   that we are unable to continue offering ''free banking'' to our customers. This recent change of policy is due to   costs, and we feel that if we are to continue to   the professional level of personal service that we have provided to our
since 1984, we must now obtain a contribution towards our   .
You will note that our charges are below the average   by the UK Clearing Banks, as we wish to remain competitive in this market.

The charges will be   to your account monthly, in   .

The minimum elegible balance requirement for those accounts which are interest bearing has been   from USD 100,000.00 or currency equivalent, to USD 50,000.00 or currency equivalent. This   in the minimum balance requirement will therefore
for some of the charges which will be paid by yourselves.

If you have any questions   the new charges, would you please telephone either myself, or my colleague, **Mr** [*name*].

Kind regards,
Yours sincerely,

Wendy Cash
Manager

Photocopiable material   © Oxford University Press 1994

13 MANAGING ACTIVITIES IN THE CLASSROOM

The management style of a teacher or trainer will depend on his or her personality, background, and experience. Equally, the trainer should be ready to make some modifications to his or her style in accordance with the needs of the learners. As already pointed out in Chapter 8, the learners' expectations of their trainer will vary with their cultural or educational background and previous job or training experience. Some learners will expect the teacher to play a dominant role in setting objectives and tasks, and in controlling their learning behaviour; others will be happier if they themselves are able to contribute to the organization of their course. Some learners expect the trainer to correct every language mistake; in some cultures, however, emphasizing a learner's mistakes may lead to a 'loss of face' and will cause severe embarrassment and resentment.

Deciding on strategies for developing a good working relationship with an individual or group is the subject of this chapter. Four key areas are considered:

1 One-to-one v. group tuition
2 Individual tasks: setting up and giving feedback
3 Role-play and simulation: setting up and giving feedback
4 Course design: putting it all together.

One-to-one v. group training

There are advantages and disadvantages to both one-to-one and group training. The choice will depend largely on how much the company is willing to pay, but also on the learner' needs. Some aspects of one-to-one and group training are compared in Tables 13.1 to 13.5, below.

Table 13.1: Trainer–learner relationships

One-to-one	Groups
If the learner expects the teacher to be dominant, he or she may be shy and defensive, and will need encouragement to speak out.	Some groups may be competitive, others co-operative. In a competitive atmosphere, shy learners will need encouragement to contribute, while strong personalities will dominate. In co-operative groups, all learners will be able to participate effectively. Use team-building activities to build co-operative skills.
The learner is involved at all times and is under stress to concentrate. He or she will become tired more quickly. It will be important to vary the pace and type of activity, and to give short breaks—for example, by setting a reading or writing task or time for general conversation, if needed.	The pace is usually faster. It is important to involve the learners by varying the types of interaction: teacher–learner/learner–learner/ use of audio or video or text as stimulus.
The learner may find it difficult to contribute a lot of ideas without stimulus from other learners. The trainer must then provide stimulus.	A lot of stimulus can come from the collective ideas and experience of group members. An effective strategy is to encourage contributions and group interactions.

Table 13.2: Activities for one-to-one and group training

One-to-one	Groups
Learner-centred activities are especially appropriate (see Chapter 11.). Any speaking tasks that involve the learner in presenting, describing, or explaining are valuable.	The time allowed for individuals to speak in monologue will be constrained by the size and patience of the group. Activities which involve learner–learner interaction are important for increasing the time that each learner can speak (pair/group work).
Role-play and simulation are possible, with the trainer playing one of the roles (two-way interaction only).	Role-play and simulations will be important elements of the course.
Discussion activities will require the trainer to take an active part (e.g. by asking for opinions, agreeing or disagreeing).	Discussion activities should be successful given good group dynamics. The teacher will be usually be in the role of observer.
If the learner does not have many ideas, brainstorming activities may not work well.	Brainstorming activities are useful for involving everybody and encouraging contributions.

Table 13.3: Materials for one-to-one and group training

One-to-one	Groups
A single coursebook is unlikely to meet all the needs of the individual, unless his or her needs are very non-specific.	A coursebook may be appropriate on some kinds of group courses.
The trainer may not need to bring many materials to the course if the learner has something specific to work on (e.g., preparing a presentation or report).	The trainer will need to be well-prepared with materials and activities for each lesson.
Supplementary materials will be useful for dealing with specific language problems or developing skills.	Supplementary materials will be useful for creating variety and changing the pace.
Audio and video materials will be important for exposing the learner to new voices and accents and for providing a change of pace.	The same is true for groups.
The trainer should be flexible in bringing in materials as needs arise.	The trainer will have to make some decisions about materials before the start of the course.

Table 13.4: Which learners benefit most from one-to-one or group training?

One-to-one	Groups
Job-experienced learners who have very specific needs.	Pre-experience or low-experience learners or learners who do not have very specific needs.
Job-experienced learners who have severe time constraints, either because their work schedule does not allow much time for training, or because they have some urgent need—e.g. a presentation, a trip abroad.	Learners who need English for interacting in meetings. Learners who need to acquire interactive skills, such as co-operating, listening, asking questions.
Learners with strong personalities who would dominate or feel frustrated trying to co-operate in a group.	Learners who work well as members of a team.
Learners who are shy of speaking in front of others.	Learners who enjoy the social aspects of being in a group.

Table 13.5: Giving feedback

One-to-one	Groups
The trainer will develop a deeper understanding of the learner's special problems.	The trainer will not know the individuals in a group as intimately as in a one-to-one situation.
It will be easier to be open with the learner with less risk of embarrassing him or her.	There will be less time and fewer opportunities to give detailed feedback.
The trainer will develop a role of counsellor or consultant in diagnosing problems, discussing them with the learner, and advising strategies.	Sensitive areas will have to be dealt with outside the classroom on a one-to-one basis.
Some of the feedback may relate to personal factors such as motivation, learning style, attitude to the course.	Individual feedback is more likely to relate directly to language problems and will deal less with learning or communication problems.
	Strategies for learning or for communicating effectively which relate to the whole group can be discussed openly.

The subject of feedback will be dealt with in more detail on pages 200–8.

Dealing with individuals

The following points apply particularly to one-to-one training in a business or professional context. For a comprehensive discussion of individual teaching, see *One to One* by Peter Wilberg (Language Teaching Publications, 1987).

– Learners are very demanding, and many wish to be pushed even though they may not say so.
– Some learners may be quiet and not forthcoming. This may be because they are tired, but it may also be that they are not used to managing themselves in a learning situation where the reins of control have been removed. In such cases the trainer has to be open and straightforward: there is nothing wrong with talking openly with the learner about the kinds of activities he or she prefers, or sees as important, and the specific content/topic areas that are deemed important—indeed this is an ongoing part of needs analysis.

– Very often a learner is undisciplined, and does not show any concrete learning strategies at all. On a short course there is little one can do to remedy that problem, but recognizing that it exists can help in the choice of material and the pacing of the course.

– A frequent complaint from learners is that they are not corrected enough. Whatever the views of the trainer on error correction, if the learner feels that insufficient attention is being paid to errors, he or she will regard the trainer's performance as inadequate. The classroom is not the time for a debate on pedagogical correctness. Systematic monitoring and feedback, and the use of the tape recorder or video, are the best ways of building a sense of progress for the learner. It is in the one-to-one course, not the group course, that the most satisfactory kind and degree of feedback can be developed. The trainer has only the one learner to consider; the learner is not compromised by correction in front of others; the course itself benefits from a mix of intensive and less intensive feedback, and a thorough variety of feedback (the sound system, vocabulary, grammatical structure, appropriacy, discourse elements, socio-cultural competence, communicative skills) that is achieved as a result of on-going dialogue and agreement of needs.

Course design and the individual learner

Unlike courses for groups, which have to be carefully planned in advance (see pages 209–14), the individual course allows for much more freedom. As a result of discussion with the learner, or observation of the learner's progress, an existing plan may be changed or rather vague ideas may be firmed up into a clear syllabus and course design. In these circumstances, it is more helpful to look at the overall mix of factors that need to be considered when creating the course for the individual, rather than setting out foolproof structures.

The following procedure is helpful for most learners:

1 Find out about the learner and his or her needs.
   – Go through any information you have about the learner and the company beforehand (questionnaires, product literature).
   – Do any background reading you need to do beforehand (about what a pathologist does, or a systems analyst, or a production manager).
   – Interview the learner during the first session in order to establish needs.
2 Choose from the following:
   – The learner needs to improve general speaking/listening skills for business purposes (meetings, telephoning, social).
   – The learner needs to improve specific speaking/listening skills for business purposes (telephoning, presentations, negotiations).
   – The learner needs to improve reading/writing skills for specific business purposes (letters, documents, reports).

3 Take account of the following:
   – Initial language level: it is easier to make noticeable improvement when the learner is at a lower level than at a higher level.
   – Age and background: it may be more difficult to raise the language level with an older learner than with a younger one.
   – Expectations: what does the learner expect of the course in terms of work-load, pace, and final performance?
   – Business needs: these will be established on the first day and as the course develops. The material and the language work should reflect those needs, and reflect the type of business environment (where possible) in which the learner works.

4 Choose from the following activities:
   – Activities which analyse accuracy with tenses and time
   – Activities which improve performance with tenses and time
   – Activities which analyse accuracy with modals
   – Activities which improve performance with modals
   – Activities which practise basic functions of rational exposition and enquiry (Wilkins, *Notional Syllabuses*, 1976), such as comparison and contrast, cause and effect, condition, result and consequence, justification, describing trends
   – Activities which practise other useful functions, such as recommending, complaining, complimenting, etc.
   – Activities which develop basic rhetorical skills, such as building up arguments, balancing points of view, putting forward opinions
   – Activities which analyse and improve accuracy with questions
   – Activities which analyse and improve performance with language relating to space (dimension, location, motion)
   – Activities which analyse and improve performance with various means of referencing (to people, to time, to objects)
   – Activities which analyse and improve the ability to make spoken/written text coherent (linking and signalling devices, appropriacy, register, consistency, development of theme)
   – Activities which analyse and improve the language of business skills (telephoning, presentations, negotiations, chairing)
   – Activities which improve interactive skills (naming topics for discussion, responding to others, developing themes)
   – Activities which develop strategies for learning, such as repair tactics ('I'll just say that again, I'm afraid I don't the name in English, but it's like a . . .')
   – Activities which help co-operation, such as repetition and clarification, rephrasing and restatement
   – Activities which promote vocabulary development
   – Activities which promote cross-cultural awareness

- Activities which analyse and improve social and survival skills
- Activities which are aimed at improving basic language skills (grammar review, grammar explanation, spelling, numbers, pronunciation)
- Activities which are aimed at developing listening skills
- Activities which are aimed at developing reading skills.

5 Take into account the following:
- How much of a mix does the learner need?
- How shall I pace the day/lesson?
- Am I giving the input that is really necessary?
- What exactly do I hope to achieve with this task?
- Have I given the learner enough time to prepare for this task?
- Does the learner know why the task is being done?
- How does this task relate to the learner's overall needs and the syllabus?
- How does this particular activity relate to other activities we are doing today, or during the course?

Some examples of learners' work

Below, we are including four short extracts of learners' work in order to show the process of setting-up, analysis, and feedback, and to emphasize the intensity of the trainer–learner relationship in individual tuition classes.

A Scandinavian telecommunications engineer (low-level)

Set-up

The learner used Framework 1 on page 134 which relates to needs analysis. The framework was explained, and the learner was given a short while to think about what he wanted to say.

> I am using the diagram you will have, and the arrow-up pointed at my boss and talk about social matters, holidays and which jobs are going on. The arrow-in persons in the company, persons clerical level, persons technical support and the personnel who do the job working as project. The arrow-out look at the owner of houses where the cables goes and persons in the community, and the down arrow we don't use because I don't have some under me.

Analysis

This short description gives the trainer a clear idea of the lines of communication. There are statements which need clarification. The 'owner of houses' means the person who owns the buildings in which sub-stations are housed, and 'the persons in the community' refers to decision makers.

The control of the sound system is poor. The speaker has problems with agreement and tense; the text is also not held together very well, either by linking words or phrases, or through the voice. The immediate impression was quite poor, although actual analysis of what was said shows that the speaker knows rather a lot of English, probably at a passive level.

This is the kind of speaker who is likely to respond well to a two-week intensive course. Apparent inaccuracies and poor projection often hide considerable passive awareness.

The speaker needs the basic faults—concordance and tense structure—pointing out, but the trainer felt that what this extract showed was not lack of correctness, or accuracy, but lack of practice.

A French financial manager (high level)

Set-up

This learner wanted to practise formal presentations and interactional language, and the short extract below is from an example of the latter. This was an exchange at the beginning of the course; it took place just after the British general election in 1992. (T = Trainer, L = Learner)

> **T** . . . especially now, with everybody considering the implications of the election.
> **L** That's right, that's right. I was in London last week during the election day, and the day after, and I registered all the reactions.
> **T** Oh, right.
> **L** Of this surprising result. Yes. Yes, it's rather strange. I don't know if this due to a mistake in the polls, or if it is due to a short term movement which is due to . . . it's interesting to listen to the reactions . . . you have to be able to, with some care, to avoid, how you say that, you say 'walking on the eggs'?

Analysis

This learner is evidently at a very high level. His interaction is very natural ('That's right, that's right'), and he is very idiomatic. With people at this level, materials need have only very bare outlines; the greatest source of material is their own experience, and this is what has to be accessed. Points for the trainer to be attentive to here are: (1) 'How you say that?'—a mistake with question forms. Very probably there will be errors or odd usage occurring because of influence from the first language ('registered', 'the eggs').

A French statistician (intermediate level)

Set-up

This learner needed practice in the language of meetings. On this occasion she was putting forward a point of view in a discussion concerning the influences of cultural differences and attitudes on management styles.

> [Talking about Japan and the United States]
> But this is due to the fact that the way of managing people seems to them more different. They, the same when they have the production in another country. But, they say that our European and American businessmen must have not this thing, when they have business with Japanese people, and I think that . . . do a lot to reconcile business people—the Americans and the Japanese—and the fact that Japan used to copies, they say we have to compete in a different way . . .

Analysis

There are few problems with vocabulary, or the willingness to try complex statements. There are problems with organization, and this is what the training should concentrate on. For example, when she says 'They, the same when they have the production in another country', it is as though her thoughts are outpacing her speech. She needs to slow down and think things through more before speaking. Organization framework materials could help her a lot. It would be a great mistake to see this problem as something merely grammatical.

A Scandinavian oil executive (high level)

Set-up

This is an extract from a formal presentation on the future of a company. The person in question is in a position of responsibility, and frequently has to speak in public.

> We have to develop the culture of the company, maybe in the direction of being more international, maybe we are going to be speaking English as the company language in the company. We have to develop people, we have to recruit people. In comparison with international oil companies we have a staff, that is, that don't have, er, without the international experience. This means we have to recruit and develop people in the meantime. The financial situation of the company may be too weak. It is a resource-demanding decision. We had to take resources and put into the development of the international part of the company, and that means we have to take resources from other parts of the company it might as interesting as this part.

But nevertheless it's a high-risk decision. It's a long-term decision. It's a resource-demanding decision. I think it's difficult to take that decision this year. The company is becoming an international company.

My conclusion is that the management of the company should develop a strategic plan within this year and present it to the board, and that within ten years from now 25 per cent of the resources of the gas and oil is located outside of this country, and that within ten years we also have production outside of this country.

Analysis

In fact, the speaker has a good command of the sound system, so that what he said sounded better than an analysis of it when written down. There are certain obvious points to look at from a grammatical point of view—tense, for example. The real problems are with linking and reference words. The word 'It' in 'It is a resource demanding decision' in fact weakens the statement because the referent is not totally clear. Speakers at this level can benefit greatly from training which focuses on the way they organize their ideas in English, and the way in which they hold them together—rather than looking at grammar at the sentence level. The implications are that attention will be to elements of discourse which are cohesive in nature—such as reference devices, lexical fields and lexical collocation, complex clauses, reference to time, general appropriacy of expression, and overall consistency of use.

Role play and simulation

Setting up the activity

Role play differs from simulation in that the participants are asked to adopt a new character who may have different attitudes and opinions from their own. For example, the learner could be given a role card which explains that he or she is a sales manager in a company which produces cosmetics, and that in the meeting which will be acted out, he or she must speak in favour of proposal X, or against proposal Y.

Role plays have to be prepared in detail in advance (there are lots of ready-made ones to be found in books or management training materials). They are suitable for mixed-interest groups and groups who do not have specific needs and they usually work better with imaginative learners who can think themselves into the role they are assigned. Pre-experience learners will be more likely to respond well to role play than job-experienced learners, perhaps because they are less likely to have strong opinions of their own.

Simulations, on the other hand, allow the learners to be themselves. There will be a situation to be acted out (a business dilemma or a problem), but they can express their own ideas and opinions as if they themselves were in the imagined situation. In this respect, simulations are easier for some personality types. Both role play and simulation can focus on a variety of business skills such as meetings, telephone calls, and social situations.

Simulations can be ready-made (as with role plays), or can be devised by the trainer for individuals or groups who have a need to deal with a specific situation. In this case, the trainer will need to get help from the learners in order to build up a credible problem with facts and figures that the learners can provide from their own experience.

In order to get this information, the trainer will need to ask a lot of questions, such as: 'What normally happens in this kind of situation?' 'Who do you discuss it with?' 'Do you meet face-to-face or discuss it on the phone?' and so on.

The following is an example of a simulation built up with a group of learners. The group (all from the same company) consists of engineering and technical staff who are responsible for purchasing equipment for their departments. They sometimes buy from foreign suppliers and need to practise negotiating skills in English.

The trainer discusses with the learners how the simulation will proceed. First, it is established that some group members will represent the suppliers (the name and nationality of the supplier company is decided by the learners, as is the type of equipment that they supply), while the others will be themselves. Second, it is established that the buyers and suppliers have had previous contact, and that a meeting has been set up to discuss the purchase of a certain type of equipment (the learners provide technical details of the equipment they want—product brochures from an actual supplier could be used here). The learners draw up a list of points that would be discussed in the negotiation—for example, price discount, payment terms, delivery arrangements, maintenance contract.

Each group (buyers and suppliers) then meets separately to prepare for the negotiation: buyers will decide what demands they will make; suppliers decide what their offer will be.

The trainer can co-ordinate this process by monitoring the discussion in each group. If it becomes apparent that more information is needed by both groups for the simulation to work, then this can be discussed by both groups together.

In both role plays and simulations (whether ready-made or created by the learners), time for preparation is essential if participants are going to play their parts successfully. They must be very familiar with the background information and must have a clear idea of what shape the interaction will have, and what they are trying to achieve.

Language preparation will also be essential. In the simulation of a buyer–supplier negotiation referred to above, the language of negotiation would have been treated earlier on the course, as would other important language, such as giving technical specifications, and comparing and contrasting.

What can go wrong?

There are many risks involved in running a role play or simulation, particularly in group teaching.

1 There is too much background information (it is time-consuming to prepare and the learners cannot keep the details in mind).

2 There is too little information (the participants have to invent it during the role-play, which can upset the course of discussion).

3 The discussion goes on too long.

4 The participants get so involved that they lose sight of the objectives (i.e. to practise certain kinds of language or behaviour).

5 The discussion becomes personal and confrontational. Individuals become so involved with arguing from a particular standpoint that it is then impossible for the group to reach a solution or a decision. (Learners often exhibit quite different behaviour in role plays from that which they would show in a real-life meeting because they know they have nothing to lose.)

6 If there is a chairperson, he or she fails to exert control and the meeting becomes chaotic.

7 Usually as a result of (6), the more confident participants dominate and others feel more and more frustrated as they are unable to contribute.

8 The participants do not listen to each other—they continue to repeat the same arguments again and again.

9 If it is a mixed nationality group, the participants may not understand each other well, or may have different attitudes concerning how a meeting (for example) should run.

Strategies for reducing the risks

1 A ready-made role play must be carefully selected, taking into consideration the level and experience of the learners. It is important to avoid complicated situations with a lot of background data if time is short, if the learners' level is too low, or experience too limited. This applies particularly for role plays which were originally created for native English speakers.

2 When preparing a role play or simulation, particularly if it has been created specially, take plenty of time to discuss it with the participants in detail: what they want to say, how they plan to back up their arguments, what they will propose and so on. Gaps in the facts may then become apparent and can either be filled, with the full knowledge of everyone, or can be disregarded as unimportant to the situation. Role plays which are used again and again can be modified in the light of experience.

3 It is vital to set a time limit for the action stage of the role play or simulation, and make sure that participants are kept aware of the time. This should discourage time-wasting. However, extra time could be allowed if it is necessary for a discussion to reach a successful conclusion.

4 It is very useful to take a break during longer role plays in order to discuss how things are going and to remind participants of language or behavioural objectives (interim feedback). The break could be decided in advance, and may occur naturally. (For example, in a negotiation role play it is normal for teams to break after demands have been made so as to discuss how they will respond to them.) If there is no obvious occasion to take a break, the trainer may decide to interrupt if things are not running smoothly.

5 In the case of meetings and negotiations, it is a good idea if, before the start, the participants are told that they must try to reach agreement. They could be reminded that a role play or simulation tries to imitate real life and that co-operation is nowadays seen as a more effective business strategy than aggression. If participants behave aggressively in the role play, this should be pointed out during interim feedback.

6 The choice of a chairperson is vital to the success of a simulated meeting. The chairperson should be someone with a good command of language and a strong enough personality to be able to take control. He or she should also be a good listener and have good clarifying and summarizing skills. If no such person can be found in the group, the trainer might consider taking the role of the chair. The chairperson (if it is a learner) should be carefully briefed on his or her role and helped to prepare an agenda or structure for the meeting. The chairperson is

responsible for keeping the meeting to its time limit, for bringing the group to a decision, and for opening and closing the meeting.

7 The chair should also control the dominant speakers and should encourage the quiet participants to contribute. If he or she does not do so, this must be pointed out during the interim feedback.

8 Before starting the role play, it is useful to remind participants that effective participation in meetings involves developing good listening skills. This principle can be reinforced during discussion practice: at some point in the middle of a discussion, stop the activity and ask individual learners: 'What was X's point of view?' 'Who else agreed?' 'Who put forward the point of view that . . .?' 'What arguments did they have?' Once learners get used to the idea that they will be asked these questions, they will start listening to each other more carefully.

9 It is always difficult to deal with problems that arise when one (or more) participants has poor pronunciation and cannot be understood by the others. Encouraging groups to be supportive and co-operative helps, but may not solve the problem completely. Make sure that the learners have plenty of practice in the use of language for clarification.

10 Dealing with different cultural attitudes to meetings can also be a thorny problem which of course mirrors real life. A good approach is to bring the problems out in the open and discuss them. Ask each of the learners to say what they think makes a successful meeting, and what they think good meetings behaviour should consist of. Put the main points on the board and then look at any differences. See if the group can accept these or find compromises.

Giving feedback

Interim feedback

This should focus on the success of the role play or simulation as a whole rather than on the performance of individuals. However, as mentioned above, it may be necessary to remind the chairperson of his or her role. A good strategy is to ask the participants to give their evaluation of the meeting so far. If there are problems that they do not mention, the trainer can add comments; on the other hand, if the learners are over-critical of themselves, the trainer can be reassuring. In general, the comments the trainer makes will focus on interaction within the group. The trainer might ask one or more participants to summarize what has been said so far. This is useful to check if the points made were well understood by the others. If there was a misunderstanding, could this have been clarified? Where there has been disagreement, what was the reaction of the other participants? If some people expressed their opinions too strongly, how did the others feel? Feedback at this stage should not deal with the language mistakes which were made, unless these gave rise to a misunderstanding. Key words (or numbers) which were expressed wrongly and which have implications for the ensuing discussion should be corrected, however. The interim feedback session should take about five minutes.

Feedback after the role play has ended

A different approach to feedback can be taken if the trainer has access to a video camera to record events. An audio cassette player can also be used but is less effective in a group situation in longer role plays (it is difficult to identify the speakers and less interesting to play back). If there is no possibility of recording the activity, the trainer must observe and take notes carefully.

The procedure below can be used when a recording has been made.

1 Immediately after the role play ends, hold a second feedback session similar to the interim feedback session. This will have the same orientation as the interim feedback and will follow up on points raised in the interim feedback (was there any improvement?). There should be plenty of positive points to make at this stage. Appraisal should relate to the learner's expected performance level, not with a hypothetical native speaker playing the same role. Major language problems can be dealt with here, but not in too much detail. This feedback session will probably take about five minutes.

2 Video or audio review could provide useful material for several subsequent sessions. Use of the video should be carefully prepared: it is tedious for the participants to sit through a re-play of the whole role play unless it is less than 10 minutes.

Although it is time-consuming, the trainer should, if possible, view the video alone and select (by counter numbers) the parts of the role play that are most interesting to play again. Extracts can be selected because a participant has used language or behaviour successfully, or because language was not used appropriately, or because an opportunity to use certain language was missed. This helps to reinforce learning. Similarly, extracts can be selected because they illustrate effective use of behaviours (checking, clarifying, summarizing) or lack of these behaviours. If someone has failed to convey information accurately, or has not understood accurately, this may also provide a point for discussion, and the trainer can suggest how communication could be improved. Small language mistakes which are due to slips and which did not affect communication should not be dwelt upon. It is unrealistic to expect learners to speak with 100 per cent accuracy during a role play: there will probably be an even higher rate of errors than normal, because the learners will have concentrated on communicating rather than on language accuracy. Errors which are due to a lack of knowledge could be taken up and explained if appropriate at this stage of the course. Vocabulary could be introduced where a word has been misused. Overall appraisal should focus on how well the learners communicated and how well they interacted with each other: these are the goals of every role play and simulation.

Below are extracts from a simulation that was carried out by two different groups. On each occasion, the simulation was set up in a different way. It is interesting to compare the language used and the overall effectiveness of the activity in each version. The situation on which the simulation is based is as follows:

A small hi-tech company runs into financial difficulties and decides that they will have to move out of London to reduce their costs on rent. A committee meets to discuss the benefits of two alternative locations: Bristol (100 miles or 160 kilometres west of London) or Livingstone (a new town near Edinburgh).

The participants have prepared and exchanged information about the two locations and have now reached the decision-making phase of the meeting, which lasted 30 minutes altogether.

Group 1
The group which participated in the first example consisted of six people: two Germans, three Spanish, and a Finn.

The two learners who were given the role of supporting Bristol are shown in the script as B1 and B2; those supporting Livingstone are shown as L1 and L2. A fifth participant is neutral (N), as is the chairperson (Ch).

Points raised in the discussion touch on the following facts which were given in the background to the role play:

- The company will have to pay a lump sum to the staff to compensate them for the move (calculated at a total of £50,000).
- Most of the staff are expert engineers who spend five months or so a year travelling abroad.
- Houses in Livingstone are about half the price of houses in London.

The extract comes after about 25 minutes of a 40-minute role play.

Feedback notes

N   The problem is we have to move—the company has to move. Who wants to stay in the company, he has to move. I agree that we build up a team—a qualified team of engineers. We need these people. It is difficult to get these people. You can find them in London, or in certain areas. But we have to move, and it doesn't matter—to Bristol or to Livingstone.

Wrong tense: should be 'We have built up'

[Several people try to interrupt here]

B1   The ideal solution for the family is not to move.

L1   But this is not the ideal solution.

The chair needed to control the interruptions.

[More interruptions and talking at once]

B1   Yes! Yes! Because you don't need to pay the £50,000 for the compensation for moving. You don't need to pay the £3,000 for the relocation . . .

B2   If the families can stay in their homes where they are now, they haven't—when they move to Bristol—they have not to move to another house near Bristol, they can stay near—in London, or where they are now.

L1   So, this is a high cost of transport for them.

B2   There is no costs.

L1   If I well understood, you mean that the people will remain in London and will go everyday to Bristol to work.

B1 uses 'Yes' because he doesn't know a better way to strengthen his argument. He could say: 'It is a good solution because . . .'

L1 draws a good conclusion here.

L1 clarifies the meaning very effectively here.

B2   You said before that most of the people are out of—are abroad.

L1   Yes, but this is not—oh . . . I mean, yes . . .

B2   So the families have not to move with the whole household to another area. They can stay in the near of London, and only the company will have to move to Bristol and er—if—er er the households will not move, you have not to pay this lump sum, only for five or six . . .

Grammatical error here: not 'have not' but 'don't have'. Good strategy to ask for reasons.

L1   Could you give me some reasons why some families could stay in the same place?

Ch   Well I think we are now in a large discussion . . .

The chairman is not strong enough in stopping the discussion. He needs a strong phrase, e.g. 'Right! Let's summarize the position so far.'

B1   [interrupts] We are people that work for this company and that is our feeling.

Ch   José, I think er . . .

L2   But you are missing one point . . .

B1   Nobody likes moving.

L2   No, I don't think so.

L2 means that he disagrees. It would be clearer if he said 'Sorry, but I disagree.'
The chairman should not respond with an opinion but should encourage him to speak and to say what he means.

Ch   But it's necessary. Yes?

[L2 shrugs, unable to find an answer.]

B1   It's necessary to move the company but the best solution would be: move the company, and not move people. Don't move the families. Yes!

B1's way of arguing is to keep repeating the same message. He doesn't give facts or reasons as back-up. 'Yes' is not a very appropriate strengthener.

[Several people start to talk at once. L2 indicates that he wants to speak. Someone says 'Ssh!'.]

L2   You are missing one point. I have here a newspaper reference. People doesn't very much agree moving. They understand that company's situation and they are ready to move.

                                                     He means that 'people don't mind moving'.

[More interruptions as others disagree.]

       Not all, but . . .

L1   But they understand the situation. The other solution is to close the company.

B1   No, the solution is . . .

B2   The solution is to move to Bristol.

L2   One point. A point. This particularly person here—he is going to get £100,000 for his home and he can buy two same kind of house in Livingstone.

                                                     'One point'—not quite English usage, but a useful way to come in.

L1   Yes.

L2   Is he going to change his mind?

L1   And if I may add something. They will receive an average of £50,000. This is very convenient for them. So this could be a way to compensate, or . . .

                                                     This idea needs to be clarified: did he mean that employees would all receive £50,000 by selling their homes or has he misunderstood how much compensation the company intends to pay?

B1   I'm not sure about this. I'm not sure if people prefer to get this—er—£50,000 of compensation and pay £50,000 for a new house—er—in the middle of nowhere.

L1   Sorry. I disagree completely. This is not in the middle of nowhere. This is the most industrialized area in—in—in Scotland, so don't . . . please be serious!

                                                     He didn't really need to say 'I disagree completely' here.

B1   In my opinion, people prefers not to move far away.

Ch	Do you think it's possible not to move people, but move the company?	*The chairperson should not be asking this question at this stage of the discussion. The*
B1	Yes! Sure!	*group has been moving round*
Ch	Do you think it's an alternative to . . .	*in circles and, at this point, they need (under the chair's leadership) to start evaluating*
B2	Then we can save a lot of this lump sum. Most of the people do not move with their households in the area of Bristol and I would suspect that you could save nearly £40,000.	*the advantages and disadvantages of the alternative proposals. A good intervention would be: 'OK. Let's see what the effects of your proposal would mean for the company.'*

Overall, we can see a number of the problems mentioned on page 198: weak chairing; one or two participants unable to make a contribution while others dominate; the participants not listening to each other, and not employing good arguing strategies. They need to have these things pointed out and then to be given the chance to try to improve their performance. Positive points can be made about some of the interventions and about the attempt of the Livingstone pair to clarify the proposal made by the Bristol pair.

Group 2

The group which participated in the second example consisted of two Swedes, a German, a French woman, and a Hungarian. The initials used to distinguish the speakers in the tapescript (T, F, K, and Z) are the first name initials of the participants. In this version, participants were not asked to support either Bristol or Livingstone, but simply to solve the problem in the best way for the company. In this extract, the chairperson controls the discussion much more strongly, and validates the points made by writing them on a flipchart under headings: Advantages for Bristol/For Livingstone, Disadvantages for Bristol/For Livingstone.

Feedback notes

Ch	What other suggestions, ideas, and topics have we to look at?—Do we have?
F	Yes. I think there is a question regarding the family—perhaps a question of quality. The family is . . .

T Schools.

F Schools and, er yes, but also regarding the moving by itself. I think the family should be less frustrated to go to Bristol rather than Livingstone. It's er also the same reason: it's near London so they are not completely less all the things they are, did, before. They can go back to London at the weekend and see friends or family or . . .

Ch So I put it on this side.

K I agree with you. That's a big favour for Bristol. It isn't good to move so far away from relatives and so on. As I can see—er—many people, many employers are not at home so very much so it's a bigger problem for the family who stays at home to have some sort of security in the relatives.

Z Just a moment. Er, the objective is to move to find a cheaper location and there is no big difference between Bristol and Livingstone— in annual, er,—two thousand or less. One hundred and five hundred—one thousand five hundred pounds per year.

Ch Which number are you looking for?

Z Annual rent and rates.

Ch Yes, this is for Bristol nineteen thousand seven hundred and . . .

Z Seven hundred, yes you told. And if I take the percentages, only in the annual salary—but I suppose there is another cost.

T The travel costs will be higher.

Z Yes, and this—this is only over five per cent in the salary. This is not a big difference. If we want to have— if we want to reduce the cost, from

T's contributions are always short. He caused some confusion with this interruption.

'not completely without'

'a big advantage'

She meant 'employees'

Z becomes confused with the figures and fails to explain his point completely.

'Which figure are you looking at?'

Again, he does not complete his argument.

He probably meant 'only about five per cent difference in salary'.

the cost point of view I say that
Bristol and Livingstone are the
same.

Ch You mean—er—did I understand
right when I say, when I try to say
in my own words that costs which
are obvious, which we have on the
paper here are nearly roughly the
same, but that we have to focus on
trip costs—costs for trips?

*The chair works hard to get at
the meaning.*

*This was T's point. Z wanted
to refer to the problem for the
families.*

Z Trip costs and some er—some
subjective er—can I say subjective
er for example . . .

*He wanted to say it was a
personal question rather than
an economic one.*

Ch Topics?

Z For family. Yes, yes, yes.

Ch So, I should put down on the paper:
Bristol for the trip costs is better
probably?

Z Sure.

Ch OK.

At the end of this simulation, the group was asked if they felt it had been successful, and if so, why? Everyone reported that they felt it had been successful because they had all had a chance to make a contribution and to have their views considered; they had reached a decision easily and without anyone feeling frustrated or isolated. The meeting had been handled efficiently and well by the chairperson and all the participants were satisfied with their performance.

Course design: putting it all together

Being able to select materials and decide on appropriate tasks and activities are skills that all teachers need to develop from the very start of their career. To acquire the art of drawing up a course plan—i.e. to achieve a good balance of activities as well as maintain a steady progression in the build-up of knowledge and skills—is a less obvious need. There are, however, many teaching situations that demand it.

If teachers follow a coursebook, or course materials already prepared by their school or institution, then much of the work of course planning will have been done for them. However, they will still need to think about what supplementary materials to bring in and when.

There are, on the other hand, many kinds of Business English courses which a general business coursebook cannot cover—for example, short intensive courses and highly-specific courses for individuals or homogeneous groups. In the case of intensive courses, a coursebook does not work because of the way in which the momentum is built up and maintained. Most coursebooks contain too much material and progress too slowly. The emphasis has to be on diagnosing needs and finding a short route to practical solutions with frequent opportunities to try out language and develop good communication strategies. In the case of very specific courses, there is unlikely to be a coursebook which will meet all the needs of the learner(s) in terms of language areas treated in an appropriate context and appropriate skills development at the right level of difficulty.

The methodology we have most strongly advocated in this book may have tended to stress the need for flexibility and awareness of the learner's requirements. Why then is course design important?

Particularly on group courses, the trainer needs to have an overall picture of what the course is about and where it is going. The long-term objectives of the learners have to be kept in mind so as to avoid time-consuming distractions and red herrings. This is important for the trainer from the point of view of managing what goes on in any lesson, and also from the point of view of the learners, who need to see why they are doing the tasks they are set, and what they are going to achieve at each stage of the course. A course plan is vital for maintaining motivation, especially on longer-term extensive courses.

The learners also need to have a variety of different kinds of activities so that their interest is maintained; and this means varying the pace as well as the focus of training and the method of practising. A good course plan should prepare for this need.

The fact that a course has been tightly planned does not imply that the trainer can no longer react flexibly to the learners' needs. It is much better to make a decision to diverge from a clear path and then return to it again than it is to wander around without a particular direction.

In order to plan a course, the trainer needs to do the following:

1 Write down three or four main performance objectives (see Chapter 5).

2 List the main language areas that need to be covered in order to achieve each of those objectives (grammatical, functional, lexical).

3 Decide in what sequence these language areas can best be dealt with— allowing for progression from easy to difficult and for a certain amount of recycling of language points.

4 Decide approximately how much time needs to be spent on each, according to how easy or difficult a particular area is, and how important it is (the time allowed can be adjusted later if necessary).

5 Decide how these areas can best be practised in order to develop the skills defined in the performance objectives.

6 Decide how to balance the time needed for introducing new language as against time for practising both new and known language—the need for practice and feedback time can rarely be over-estimated.

The following outlines give some ideas for approaching the task of course design for a group of learners.

An intensive general Business English course plan

Start of course

Do the group members know each other?
Yes
The learners could introduce each other to the trainer.

No
Start with brief introductions.

Learners could interview each other in pairs and afterwards report back to the group.

Could use a 'fun' group activity where learners have to interact with each other in English. This breaks down barriers, encourages co-operation, and focuses on interactive skills. It also helps the trainer to identify the training gap.

Next one or two sessions

Use these to review basic language areas. Choose language that will be useful later in the course, for example, numbers, spelling, describing the job, describing the company, asking questions, exchanging information, and clarifying information. These early sessions should not put learners under too much stress, but should help to build confidence in speaking and listening.

Is the course held in an English-speaking country?

Yes

If necessary, provide input and practice in survival English: the money, where to find banks, etc., opening and closing times, polite requests.

No

Could include a session on social English: language for meeting people from other countries, with (at a higher level) discussion of cross-cultural aspects.

The middle days

It is good to have a 'shape' to the day. Below are two examples of plans for the middle days of intensive courses:

Example 1   (low to intermediate)

Language review
Review direct question forms

New language input
Listening/reading
Introduce indirect questions (polite forms)
Introduce telephone language: listening to model, identifying language

Short practice activities
Pairwork practice: telephone language

(LUNCH)

Output activities
Role-play, simulation, presentations, projects, games, writing, etc.
Telephone role-plays: asking for information on the phone.

or

Extensive listening
Video or guest speaker

Follow-up
Discussion

Final session
Something completely different, e.g. social English, game, or discussion.

Example 2   (intermediate to advanced)

Language review
Discussion language using a short activity, conditionals

New language input
Introduce language for forecasting (expressing possibility, probability): listening to model

Short practice activities
Practise conditionals

Extensive listening
Video: documentary looking at the future

Follow-up
Discussion

Output activities
Problem-solving activity: evaluating different courses of action ('What might happen if we do this?').

End of course

It would be appropriate to have a general review of language covered during the course, or even a test.

There could also be a 'grand finale' activity: for example, presentations, or a simulation of a meeting or a negotiation, or a role play with feedback.

Another possibility would be a 'fun' activity, such as a game, a debate, or a discussion, plus advice from the trainer on how the learners can maintain or improve their language skills after the end of the course.

Finally, collect feedback from the participants about the course.

An extensive general Business English course plan

The same approach can be used to start and finish the course as on an intensive course, although the length of time given to the activities may be different.

As with intensive courses, a general shape or pattern for each session is useful. Below is an example of a lesson plan, based on a 60-minute session.

Start

Short, lively activity to get participants to relax and start thinking in English (5 minutes).

Review language from previous session(s) (5–10 minutes). This is important to show that sessions are linked and progressive.

Middle

Introduce new language: listening/reading (20 minutes)

Practice exercises (10 minutes)

Finish

Transfer activity: short role-play/discussion or game (15–20 minutes)

These activities should recycle language from previous sessions as well as practising language introduced in the present one. There should thus be a build-up of strands of language which continually recombine and interlace.

Some sessions may be completely different from the pattern, however. For example, they may be entirely taken up by role-play, a video, project work, or presentations. This helps to create variety.

Specific Business English course plans

Example 1

A three-day course for a group of six, all working in the marketing department of a pharmaceuticals company and mainly needing presentation skills.

Day 1

Introduction to the course

Discussion activity: spending on advertising

Language review: tenses; handling numerical data

Video: example of a presentation

Input on presentation language and organization

Reading and language review based on the company report

Day 2

Describing trends: listening activity and language study

Giving reasons and causes

Short presentations by the participants presenting a chart or graph

Input on forecasting and predicting

Discussion activity: future trends in pharmaceutical marketing

Day 3

Long presentations by the participants: job-related topics

Feedback and analysis of presentations

Language review

Summary of course

Example 2

A five-day course for an in-company group comprising finance and accounting staff with needs for reading (memos and instructions), letter writing, telephoning, and some social skills for receiving visitors.

Monday
Greetings and introductions
Asking questions and clarifying information
Telephoning: getting through to the person you want
Video: *Data Insecurity* episode 1
Talking about accounts: the income statement and balance sheet
Letter writing

Tuesday
Talking about cost, amount, and quantity
Describing your company
Telephoning: taking messages
Video: *Data Insecurity* episode 2
Writing skills: linking sentences and organizing information
Social English: conversation

Wednesday
Language of reporting: comparing and contrasting
Giving instructions
Telephone simulation: giving instructions
Video: *Data Insecurity* episode 3
Foreign banks and international payments
Discussion language

Thursday
The language of reporting: changes and trends
Giving instructions in writing
Reading and information exchange task
Video: *Data Insecurity* episode 4
Social English: entertaining a visitor

Friday
Language review
Reading and information exchange task
Video: *Data Insecurity* final episode
Role play: receiving visitors
Outstanding questions and summary of course

14 CURRENT TRENDS IN BUSINESS ENGLISH

This final chapter considers some of the current trends and concerns in teaching English to business and professional people. It is important to stress again a point made at the beginning of this book—namely that we have used the term 'Business English' to cover the English that is taught to a wide range of professional people, and people still in full-time education preparing for a business career. Within this range we find people with commercial jobs, research jobs, and very technical jobs—for example, in refineries or the computer field—as well as people working at management level. The issues referred to below must be seen in relation to people in all these areas, and in other professional (non-business) areas.

Language training v. skills training

One of the questions which is often debated among Business English teachers is: are we teaching language or skills? As we have seen, Business English courses often focus on such areas as meetings, presentations, and negotiations: areas which are also addressed in management skills training (usually in the mother tongue), where behavioural strategies and techniques play an important role. Many teachers feel that they do not have the expertise and should not be concerned with matters beyond teaching the language; whilst others have been keen to move into new fields and develop themselves professionally.

Our own opinion is that there are certain aspects of skills training which are better addressed in the first language and which can be taught without attention to the language being used. Equally, there are aspects of meetings, negotiations, and presentations where it is difficult or indeed impossible to focus on language without some consideration of the skills involved. Table 14.1 (overleaf) highlights the interrelationship between skills and language.

Table 14.1: Skills training v. language training

	Skills training	**Language training**
Presentations	Use of visual aids	Referring to visual aids
	The content matter of the introduction	Organizing the content of the introduction
	The content matter of the body	Organizing the content of the body, including signals and link words
	The content matter of the conclusion	Organizing the content of the conclusion
	Rhetorical skills: putting forward views	Handling rhetorical skills in the second language
	Balancing arguments	
	Style	Choosing language for the style
	Tactical questioning and tactical handling of questions	Using appropriate forms in the second language to achieve tactical ends
	Body language	
Meetings	Relationship building	Using appropriate forms of the second language to be polite, avoid offence, and create the right climate
	Chairing skills	Using the second language clearly and appropriately to control the meeting
	Rhetorical skills: putting forward views, balancing arguments, introducing ideas, drawing conclusions	Using the second language clearly and appropriately to participate in the meeting
	Listening skills	Developing listening skills in English
	Participating and co-operative skills	Using the second language for interaction, support, questioning. Using the second language to restate, reformulate, summarize.
	Body language	
	Tactical moves	

	Skills training	**Language training**
Negotiations	(In addition to the above)	(In addition to the above)
	Relationship building, including cross-cultural considerations	Using appropriate forms of the second language to build a relationship effectively
	Establishing the ground: agreeing objectives, agreeing procedure	Using appropriate forms of the second language to achieve tactical ends
	Establishing options	
	Bidding and offering	Developing sufficiently good command of the second language to interact with clarity and precision
	Bargaining and stating conditions	
	Formal summarizing and concluding	
	Establishing agreement	

The implication is that while the language trainer need not feel that he or she is teaching skills, attention has to be paid to the way the learner uses language in order to achieve particular ends. This will include attention to structure (if thought necessary), to projection and authority, to clarity, and to appropriacy. In so doing, the language trainer does not have to

approach a course from the point of view of setting out the stages of a negotiation and developing the participants' skill at negotiating by getting them to become manipulators of these stages. But the language trainer does have to know what these stages are, otherwise there will be no focus in the language training, and the learners may be unable to relate what they have learned to the real situations in which they should apply it. If in relating the teaching of English to the skills of negotiation the teaching of English is improved, then it can be argued that the language trainer is also a negotiations trainer—but always first a language trainer.

The influence of management training

A major trend in EFL generally is a growing awareness of the importance of teacher development. Part of this development involves finding out how learners learn. There is now much more cross-reading between disciplines and the value of studying behaviour theory and the psychology of learning is more appreciated among language teachers. Books such as Honey and Mumford's *Manual of Learning Styles*, written about learning and teaching styles, have attracted the attention of many EFL trainers.

In the field of business skills and management training, considerable research has been carried out into how people learn most effectively. There has been a move towards experiential learning, for example, where learners develop awareness of new concepts through active participation in tasks.

A number of business games and simulations which have been created as a vehicle for experiential learning of management skills are now being used in some Business English courses for language training. They are attractive to Business English teachers because they are well-designed, easy to use and offer interesting task material.

It is likely that this trend will continue and that, as management and business skills training develops, Business English teachers will borrow ideas, techniques and materials and incorporate them in their courses.

Methodologies

The Business English, or Professional English, environment is far-ranging and eclectic. As trainers operate in many different countries and cultural backgrounds, and have themselves many different views on teaching, it is not surprising that one can find just about every kind of methodology in the field of teaching Business English.

There is no one 'best' methodology—any teaching situation is an inter-action between the learner, the trainer (or teacher or facilitator), and the activity itself. There are certain countries and certain groups in those countries where one particular approach may work well. Equally, with another group in that country, or with a group from another background, it may not work so well, or may work badly.

The question is not 'Is Suggestopedia a good methodology?', or 'Is it right to give grammar rules?'. The question is 'What is right for this group, or this individual?'. There may be several good choices, but there may be only one choice which is right for the particular mix of learner, trainer, and any other factors that may be important.

As a general rule, hard-line supporters of particular methodologies as exclusive tools will not be able to respond to the wider ranges of learning environments that exist within the field of Business English. Methodo-logies which put the learner at the centre of the learning process are likely to be the most effective when working with professional people — particularly job-experienced learners.

Cross-cultural awareness

Awareness of the importance of one's own culture in relation to those of others has become a growing issue in the field of Business English. This trend mirrors awareness in the business field of different management styles, and different attitudes and expectations as a result of varying cul-tural influences. It is not yet clear just how much this will affect develop-ments in terms of training within the context of Business English. It is probable, however, that cross-cultural differences as a topic for discussion will become increasingly common.

From the trainer's point of view, there are two reasons why an under-standing of cross-cultural differences could be important. The first is that, inside the language classroom, differences in culture can affect relation-ships and interactions. A native-speaker trainer working abroad, or in his or her own country but teaching mixed nationality groups, is going to encounter different attitudes and behaviours and must develop ideas about how to manage these differences sensitively. The second is that the trainer may want to prepare the learners for communicating internation-ally, especially where the learners have not travelled much, or have not met many people from outside their own culture.

In the second case, some trainers may feel tempted to try some of the case studies, role-plays, and simulations that have been developed specific-ally for cross-cultural awareness training. We would, however, remain sceptical about the value of these activities in the language classroom unless they relate directly to the objectives agreed in advance by the sponsoring organization and unless the trainers have a lot of knowledge and experience in this field.

For those who wish to pursue their interests in cross-cultural awareness further, certain titles are listed in the Appendix.

Growing professionalism

As Business English teaching develops in terms of diversity, richness, and depth, the demands placed on the teacher are ever increasing. Some trainers may find a particular niche in which to specialize, while others may prefer to meet the challenges of teaching a wide variety of learners from different jobs, cultures, and educational backgrounds. As we hope to have stressed in this book, the first requirement for any Business English trainer is to be an expert in language teaching; the second requirement is to develop awareness of the needs and concerns of businesspeople and to become flexible enough to respond to those needs. This professional development is ongoing throughout a trainer's career and there is no room for complacency at any stage.

We hope that this book will play a part in contributing to trainers' professionalism whatever field they are working in and whether they are already experienced or not. Our ultimate aim is to bring a higher recognition and status to our profession and to see Business English trainers reaping greater rewards in terms of their own job satisfaction as well as increasing the value placed on them by companies, educational establishments, and employers everywhere.

GLOSSARY

course objectives: The goals of a course in English, as indicated by the *needs analysis,* and expressed in terms of what the learner should be able to do. This may include success in an examination or test, or an improved ability to operate at work in English.

extensive training: A term applied to courses which are carried out over a period of weeks or months, usually for one to three hours per week on a regular basis. Contrast *intensive training.*

feedback: The evaluation given by a trainer to a learner at the end of a task, during a course, or at the end of a course, focusing on the learner's strengths and weaknesses in language performance. It can also refer to the evaluation of training.

gambits: Formulaic expressions used to indicate the purpose of what someone is about to say. Examples could be 'I suggest . . .' or 'What about . . .' to indicate a suggestion.

in-company training: Training courses organized by a company for its staff at the company's expense. The training may be carried out on company premises, or residentially in hotels.

intensive training: A term applied to courses which are carried out during a short period of time, varying from a single day to a couple of weeks or more. Training will normally last the whole day. Contrast *extensive training.*

job analysis: The methods used to obtain a detailed description of a learner's job (or learners' jobs) with particular regard to the use of English in the job.

job-experienced: Learners who have already worked in a certain job for at least a few months. They are able to define their language needs in terms of that experience, and to exploit their knowledge and skills in language learning tasks in the classroom. Contrast *pre-experience.*

learning style: An individual approach to acquiring skills or information which can be described or characterized according to well-accepted norms.

meetings: Formal or informal discussions between two or more people which are scheduled for a specific time and place. They would normally be held for the purpose of giving or exchanging information, discussing ideas, planning, reaching decisions or solving problems.

needs analysis: A method of obtaining a detailed description of a learner's needs (or group of learners' needs). It will take into account the specific purposes for which the learner will use the language, the kind of language to be used, the starting level, and the target level which is to be achieved. The information could be obtained from a range of different people: company staff, trainers, and the learners themselves. It will have implications for the approach to training that will be taken.

negotiating: A well-established system (or set of systems) for achieving agreement which may be mutually beneficial between parties who have separate and individual goals.

performance objective: One of the goals of training defined in terms of an improvement in a specific skill such as being able to participate in meetings or to receive visitors to a company.

pre-experience: Learners who have not previously worked in any kind of job. Generally they will still be undergoing full-time education.

presentation: A pre-planned, prepared, and structured talk which may be given in formal or informal circumstances to a small or large group of people. Its objective may be to inform or to persuade.

skills training: Language instruction which specifically addresses the behaviour of learners in business-oriented skills such as report-writing, giving presentations, negotiating.

teacher: A person who imparts knowledge or information about a subject and is primarily concerned with the education and personal development of the learners in their charge. Contrast *trainer.*

trainer: A person who enables learners to develop their skills within the context of their profession. Contrast *teacher.*

training gap: The difference between the starting level and the level which the learner needs to reach in order to perform in a job. It is not necessarily the level which he or she will reach at the end of a course.

transactional: A term used to describe language which has an immediate and well-defined purpose.

BIBLIOGRAPHY

BBC/ELTDU. 1972. *English for Business/Bellcrest File.* Oxford: Oxford University Press.

Carroll, B. 1982. *Testing Communicative Performance.* Oxford: Pergamon Press.

Carroll, B. and **P. J. Hall.** 1985. *Make your own Language Tests: A Practical Guide to Writing Language and Performance Tests.* Oxford: Pergamon Press.

Council of Europe. 1992. *The Threshold Level 1990.* London: HMSO.

English Language Teaching Development Unit. 1975. *Stages of Attainment Scale.* Oxford: Oxford University Press.

Firth, J. 1971. *British Banking.* London: Cassell.

Greenall, S. 1986. *Business Targets.* Oxford: Heinemann.

Grice, H. P. 1975. 'Logic and conversation' in P. Cole and J. L. Morgan (eds.): *Syntax and Semantics III, Vol. 3: Speech Acts.* New York: Academic Press, pp. 41–58.

Hollett, V. 1991. *Business Objectives.* Oxford: Oxford University Press.

Honey, P. and **H. Mumford.** 1992 (new edition). *A Manual of Learning Styles.* Maidenhead: P. Honey.

Kellor, E. 1979. 'Gambits: conversational strategy signals' *Journal of General Pragmatics* 3: 219–38.

Knowles, P. and **F. Bailey.** 1987. *Functioning in Business.* Harlow: Longman.

Knowles, P. L., F. Bailey, and **R. Jillet.** 1991. *Functioning in Business* (second edition). Harlow: Longman.

Mole, J. 1990. *Mind your Manners.* London: Industrial Society Press.

Nolan, S. and **W. Reed.** 1992. *Business English Teachers' Resource Book.* Harlow: Longman.

Pilbeam, A. 1979. 'The Language Audit'. *Language Training* 1/2.

Wilberg, P. 1987. *One to One.* Sussex: Language Teaching Publications.

Wilkins, D. A. 1976. *Notional Syllabuses.* Oxford: Oxford University Press.

Williams, M. 1988. 'Language taught for meetings and language used in meetings: Is there anything in common?' *Applied Linguistics* 9/1: 445–58.

APPENDIX

Suggestions for further reading

1 Companies and Language Training

Embleton, D. and **S. Hagen.** 1992. *Languages for Business: a Practical Guide.* Sevenoaks: Hodder and Stoughton.

This book deals with language training for companies in the UK, rather than English for companies in non-English-speaking countries. It is useful for gaining insights into company needs and perceptions.

Inman, M.E. 'Corporate Language Strategies for Global Markets'. *Language Training* 10/4.

Pilbeam, A. 1991. 'Corporate Language Training in the 1990s'. *Language Training* 12/1.

Rasanen, A. 'Matching individual and corporate needs'. *Language Training* 12/2.

These articles provide a good overview of company needs and how training organizations can react to them.

2 English for Specific Purposes

Hutchinson, T. and **A. Waters.** 1987. *English for Specific Purposes—A Learning-centred Approach.* Cambridge: Cambridge University Press.

Robinson, P. 1990. *ESP Today.* Hemel Hempstead: Prentice-Hall.

These books provide a good account of approaches and strategies for ESP teaching, although they refer mainly to teaching pre-experience learners in colleges and universities, and not much is specific to Business English.

3 Syllabus and course design

Nunan, D. 1988. *Syllabus Design*. Oxford: Oxford University Press.

Yalden, J. 1987. *Principles of Course Design for Language Teaching*. Cambridge: Cambridge University Press.

This book gives a good account of how to set about analysing and identifying the language to be taught. Although it does not refer specifically to Business English, the approach advocated will be effective for Business English learners.

4 Using computers and videos for language teaching

Jones, C. and **S. Fortescue.** 1987. *Using computers in the language classroom*. Harlow: Longman.

This book gives more information on using computers for language teaching and makes many helpful suggestions on finding and creating materials.

Lonergan, J. 1984. *Video in language teaching*. Cambridge: Cambridge University Press.

This book gives information on using video for language teaching with helpful ideas for how to exploit different kinds of video material.

Stempleski, S. and **B. Tomalin.** *Video in Action*. Hemel Hempstead: Prentice Hall.

5 Dictionaries

Adam, J. H. 1985. *Longman Concise Dictionary of Business English*. Harlow: Longman.

This provides useful definitions for most of the terms commonly used in the world of business and economics.

Bannock, G., R. E. Baxter, and **R. Rees.** 1985. *The Penguin Dictionary of Economics*. Harmondsworth: Penguin.

This book is aimed at native speakers and provides definitions for terms and concepts relating to economic theory.

International Chamber of Commerce. 1985. *Key Words in International Trade*. Netherlands: Van Boekhoven Bosch.

Perry, F. E. 1979. *A Dictionary of Banking*. Plymouth: McDonald and Evans.

Very clear definitions of banking terms, including wider definitions of key concepts.

Tuck, A. (ed.) 1993. *Oxford Dictionary of Business English for Learners of English*. Oxford: Oxford University Press.

An up-to-date dictionary aimed at language learners, which provides useful definitions, plus tips on usage and pronunciation.

6 Business English reference books

Brieger, N. and **J. Comfort**. 1992. *Language Reference for Business English*. Hemel Hempstead: Prentice-Hall.

Strutt, P. 1992. *Longman Business English Usage*. Harlow: Longman.

7 Books on cross-cultural awareness

Adler, N. 1986. *International Dimensions of Organisational Behaviour*. Boston: Kent.

Damen, L. 1987. *Culture Learning: The Fifth Dimension in the Language Classroom*. Massachusetts: Addison-Wesley.

Holland, D. and **N. Quinn**. 1987. *Cultural Models in Language and Thought*. Cambridge: Cambridge University Press.

Harris, P.R. and **R. T. Moran**. 1987. *Managing Cultural Differences*. Houston: Gulf Publishing.

8 Journals

Language and Intercultural Training (formerly called *Language Training*). Language Training Services, Bath.

This journal focuses specifically on language training for companies. Subscription address: LTS, 5 Belvedere, Lansdown Road, Bath, Avon BA1 5ED, UK.

English for Specific Purposes. New York: The American University.

This encompasses a broader spectrum of specific language training. Editorial offices: ELI, University of Michigan, 2001 N. University Building, Ann Arbor, MI 48109, USA.

9 Business textbooks

Black, R. 1987. *Getting Things Done*. London: Michael Joseph.

Chapman, E. N. 1980. *Improving Relations at Work*. London: Kogan Page.

Drucker, P. 1990. *The New Realities*. London: Mandarin.

Examines political and economic issues over the coming years, and their implications for business and society.

Handy, C. 1992. *Understanding Organizations.* Harmondsworth: Penguin.

An examination of organisational structure and culture, and the role of people in organisations, with some interesting extracts from other research.

Harris, T. A. 1973. *I'm OK – You're OK.* London: Pan.

Harvey-Jones, J. 1988. *Making it Happen.* London: Fontana.

The sections on the roles of the chairperson and the board are especially useful.

Mulligan, J. 1988. *The Personal Management Handbook.* London: Warner.

Peters, T. J. and **R. H. Waterman.** 1983. *In Search of Excellence: Lessons from America's Best-run Companies.* London: Harper and Row.

An examination of key factors leading to success in a selection of American companies.

Winston, S. 1989. *Organised Executive: New Ways to Manage Time, Paper and People.* London: Kogan Page.

Suggestions for further viewing

1 Videos designed for Business English learners

Oxford University Press
Business Assignments
Meeting Objectives

Longman
Visitron: Presentations
Visitron: Negotiations

Cambridge University Press
International Business English Video

BBC
The Bellcrest File (with Oxford University Press)
Bid for Power
The Sadrina Project
The Carsat Crisis
Starting Business English

York Associates The York Training Packs:
Effective Presentations
Effective Meetings

2 Videos designed for management training and adapted for language training:

LTS/Melrose
Systems One
The Project
(Available from LTS—see address above under Journals.)

LTS/TV Choice
The Corporation
Data Insecurity

3 Authentic video sources

Management training films

Melrose Film Productions Ltd.
16 Bromells Road, London, SW4 OB4, UK

Video Arts
205 Wardour Street, London, W1

TV Choice Video Productions
27 Swinton Street, London, WC1X 9NW, UK

BBC Training Videos
Woodlands, 80 Wood Lane, London, W12 0TT, UK

Give and Take (getting the most from your meetings)
Speak for Yourself
The Troubleshooter Series

Educational films

Thames TV
Seymour Mews House, Seymour Mews, Wigmore Street, London, W1H 9PE, UK
The Square Mile

The Stock Exchange
Information and Press Department, London, EC2N 21HP, UK
My Word is my Bond
The Stock Exchange and You
The Unlisted Securities Market
The Gilt-Edged Market
Traded Options

Banking Information Service
10 Lombard Street, London, EC3V 9AT, UK

4 Television and radio

BBC World Service radio

For frequencies and times of English-language broadcasts, consult:
BBC Worldwide, P.O. Box 765, Bush House, The Strand, London WC2B 4PH, UK

BBC World Service television

Broadcasts hourly news as well as current affairs and documentary series including business topics.

For details of how to receive World Service Television in your country, and for programme schedules, contact:

BBC World Service Television Ltd., Woodlands, 80 Wood Lane, London W12 0TT, UK.

Details of schedules are also published in many local newspapers.

Europe, Middle East, South East Asia, and Indian sub-continent
General enquiries: Tel: (+44) (0)81 576 2719 Fax: (+44) (0)81 576 2782
Scheduling enquiries: Tel: (+44) (0)81 576 2751

Asia and Africa
General enquiries: Tel: (+44) (0)81 576 2248/2102 Fax: (+44) (0)81 743 9256
Scheduling enquiries: Tel: (+44) (0)81 576 2751 Fax: (+44) (0)81 743 9931

Business English examinations

Spoken English for Industry and Commerce (SEFIC), English for Business, English for Commerce
London Chamber of Commerce and Industry, Languages Section, Marlowe House, Station Road, Sidcup, Kent DA15 7BJ, UK

SEFIC is an oral exam only, although it can be taken in conjunction with the English for Business written exam. SEFIC can be taken at four levels: Preliminary, Threshold, Intermediate, and Advanced, which are defined in general performance terms.

Oxford International Business English Certificate (OIBEC)
University of Oxford Delegacy of Local Examinations, Ewert House, Ewert Place, Summertown, Oxford, OX2 7BZ, UK

This is a totally task-based exam aimed at executives (or professionals at executive level) who need English for a wide variety of business situations.

It can be taken at two levels (First level and Executive level). It covers speaking, reading, writing, and listening.

Test of English for International Communication (TOEIC)
Educational Testing Service, PO Box 6155, Princeton, NJ 08541-6155, USA

This is a multiple-choice test that includes a listening, a reading, and a sentence-completion section.

Carroll, B. *The Business English Test*
Language Training Services (for address see LTS under Journals)

This test was designed for company use and the listening and reading sections can be set and scored by non-natives with no language teaching background. There is also a writing test and guidelines for assessing oral performance. Scoring provides an assessment on a five-point scale.

Certificate in English for International Business and Trade
UCLES/RSA, RSA Exam Board:
1 Hills Road, Cambridge, CB1 2EU, UK

Performance scales

Useful scales for measuring the attainment and performance of Business English learners are available from:

British Council, IELTS Unit, English Language Division, Medlock Street, Manchester M15 4AA, UK.

LTS Training and Consulting 5 Belvedere, Lansdown Road, Bath BA1 5ED, UK.

Professional associations

IATEFL (International Association for Teachers of English as a Foreign Language).

Within IATEFL, you can join the Business English Special Interest Group (BESIG).

Apply to: IATEFL, Kingsdown Chambers, Whitstable Kent CT5 1DJ, UK.

TESOL (Teachers of English to Speakers of Other Languages)

1600 Cameron Street, Suite 300, Alexandria, VA 22314-2751, USA.

A worldwide teachers' organization based in the USA with branches in many countries. Useful for networking.

Business skills training materials: sources

Melrose
(see address under videos)

Gower-Northgate Training
Gower Publishing Company Ltd., Gower House, Croft Road, Aldershot, Hants. GY11 3HR, UK

Union Bank of Switzerland
PO Box, CH-0121, Zurich.
A useful source of banking-related information.

INDEX

Entries relate to the Introduction, Chapters 1 to 14, the glossary, and the appendices. References to the glossary are indicated by 'g' after the page number.